The Harley-Davidson and Indian Wars

The

ALLAN GIRDLER

Crestline titles are also available at discounts in bulk quantity for industrial or sales-promotional use. For details, please contact: Special Sales Manager at MBI Publishing Company, 400 First Avenue North, Suite 300, Minneapolis, MN 55401 USA.

For more books on Harley-Davidson and Indian motorcycles, visit us online at www.motorbooks.com.

ISBN 978-0-7603-3598-7

Front cover: The difference in company vision is demonstrated by these two bikes, a Harley-Davidson Knucklehead and an Indian Four. The high-profile, technologically superior Four was beat out by the proven twin on the sales floor. *Jeff Hackett*

On the frontispiece: The Indian Four, a highly celebrated model that began life as the Ace-Four. *Jeff Hackett*

On the title page: Johnny Gibson (5) and Don Hawley (88) battle at Gardena Stadium in the 1950s. *Walt Mahonydt*

On the back cover: Don Hawley (88), Bob Shirey (46), and Chuck Basney (37) dicing at Gardena Stadium

Printed in China

Contents

Acknowledgments

Just about the time I began researching this book, a guy came up to me at the races and said he liked my work, except don't I and the other historians sort of, well, rewrite the same stuff, over and over?

Um yeah, I said, sort of. If the first history book says Washington was the first president, that means the second book has to say the same thing. Can't help it, not without making up facts.

I could admit that, because I'd been learning all kinds of new history and new and surprising answers to questions that hadn't been asked before. By pretending I hadn't read the book, I found people who were there while the history was being made. And I came up with stories that didn't match what I expected to find, as you'll see on the following pages.

Who were these history-making men? In the order they turn up on my source list, which isn't in order of importance; thanks to Steve Wright, Ed Kretz, Jr., Max Bubeck, Bob Stark, Bill Tuman, Erwin Smith, Jerry Greer, George Yarocki, Lex and Everett du Pont, Gordy Clark, Doc Sucher, Don Emde, Otis Chandler, Jim Davis, Len Andres, Bill Bagnall, Allan Carter, Jerry Hatfield, Glen Bator, Dave Edwards, and David Hansen. Without their help, I couldn't have written this book.

But two men, both sadly now gone, provided the key factors here, the new insights and the history that hasn't yet been in the books: Hap Alzina and Paul du Pont. This book is dedicated to their work, their faith in the business and the sport, their trust in their fellows, and their memories. As I hope the following account proves, without Hap Alzina and Paul du Pont, there would have been no story to tell.

This snapshot turned up in a collection owned by Jerry Greer. He got it from a man who walked into Greer's Indian Engineering one day. The man's father ran a motorcycle shop in Greer's location 40 years before Greer arrived. The man offered Greer his father's scrapbook, which is where this photo came from. This means we don't know who this kid is. In the sense and spirit of our rivalry, this kid could be me, Allan Girdler. Back in 1954, when I was 17, I bought a Harley-Davidson which was three years older than me. I rigged it with secondhand parts, I was a scrawny kid in floppy t-shirt and rolled-up jeans, and I don't have a picture because I hid the bike in a neighbor's barn and my folks didn't know about it. That don't make no never mind, though, because deep down where it counts and forget that I now race the Super Senior Veteran Master Vintage class, this kid is me. You, too, I bet. *Jerry Greer*

*M*ax Bubeck, who will go on to build the fastest-ever unstreamlined Indian, can't believe he's just lost to a Harley-Davidson. *Max Bubeck*

Introduction

Armando Magri and Max Bubeck have been friends for 60 years. They have a lot in common: both have been motorcycle enthusiasts since they were kids. Bubeck built and sold engines, Magri was a dealer. Both are comfortably retired and spend their well-earned leisure hours restoring and repairing old machines.

With one big difference: Armando Magri has a collection of Harley-Davidsons. Max Bubeck's shop is packed with Indians.

So one day the old motorcycle enthusiasts—pause for chuckle at the play on words—were on a vintage rally or road run. They spent the morning riding in close company, Armando on his Knucklehead 61, Max on the 1939 Indian Four with hundreds of thousands of miles on the odo.

They came to a fuel stop. "Max," said Armando with a barely suppressed smile, "every time you pass me on that Four, I think it's a Volkswagen Bug."

Ouch. Strong words. Back on the road, Max thought about the put-down, and when they stopped for lunch, he was ready.

"I guess," he deadpanned, "you Harley riders have had a lot of practice getting passed by Volkswagen Bugs."

At the very least, the score was even, meaning even as we speak the old pals are planning their next exchange.

There is something in this rivalry, Harley-Davidson vs. Indian, that has kept it alive for two generations longer than common sense would predict.

Harley vs. Indian has been, as you will see in the course of this saga, the longest, fiercest, and best feud in the history of sport.

No? Try another. Yankees and Dodgers? They don't live there any more. Ford against Ferrari? Lasted a couple of seasons. Ford against Chevy? Closer, but in the races both brands use the same components. American's Cup? True for lots of years, but nowadays Australians skipper American boats, Americans sail for the Italians and Japanese and design for New Zealand, and the first thing the New Zealand skipper does when his team wins is move to San Diego. Hired guns, is what that is now. And anyway, when was the last time you saw a Dodgers or NZ-36 tattoo?

Nope, the prize goes to Harley vs. Indian. For 50 years, from when Harley-Davidson went into business until the Indian team shut down, the two makers, their dealers, and especially their riders, fans, and customers fought it out on the track, in the showroom, and on the drawing board. Principles were at stake, along with jobs and careers, and actions were based on honor as well as narrow self-interest and yes, knavery and deceit.

That applies to both sides. Perhaps the best part of this story is that there is no villain and no hero, not from the sidelines, anyway. Nor does it matter that Harley is today a thriving example of survival in the face of adversity while Indian is history. What matters is that nearly a century ago two sets of people, very alike and very different at the same time, drew a line between two brands of motorcycle and said, almost in so many words, Indians on this side, Harleys on the other.

Then they waved the flag or dropped the puck or threw the raw meat into the cage. . .

. . . this is the story of what happened after that.

Chapter One

Founding Fathers

The Dynamic Duo vs. the Founding Fathers

The groundwork for the Harley-Davidson/ Indian feud begins with the official invention of the motorcycle by Gottlieb Daimler, in Germany, in 1885. The best part of the legend, too good to research in case it's not so, is that Mr. Daimler had his teenage son take the first test ride. They waited until Mrs. Daimler was out of town. She came home early, in time to see her kid come wobbling down the road. She was so mad that her husband and son didn't try the machine again for a month. Sounds like now, eh?

The important part, though, was that Daimler's device, two great big wheels fore and aft, the engine between them with the rider astride, and two smaller wheels outboard to keep the rig upright, worked. It proved that an internal combustion engine could be both small enough and powerful enough to propel itself and carry a useful load. The game was underway.

Enter the Bicycle

Before the motorcycle, in terms we'd apply now, came the bicycle. Two-wheeled, self-powered transportation was the answer to a dream. The first examples, the ones the rider pushed with his feet and the ones with the giant wheel trailed by the tiny wheel, were merely popular. Then came pneumatic tires, sprockets, chains, and pedals, and the civilized world went wild. Imagine rock 'n roll, the Internet, and backward baseball caps all arriving at the same time.

This was an age of tremendous innovation, invention, and expansion. People were suddenly more prosperous than ever before, which meant the expansion of leisure time and sports

One of the beneficiaries was bicycle racing. There was cross-country competition and banked ovals, the latter involving specialized machines. Daimler's device is credited as being the first motorcycle, but there was a cascade of development prior to Daimler that grew directly out of and borrowed from bicycle technology.

In strict historical fact, the proto-bike would have been something called a "dandy-horse," a pair of straddled wheels propelled by feet that was patented in 1818. As soon as this patent was granted, there were suggestions that the machine could be powered by sails, carbon dioxide gas, clockwork springs, compressed air, or even steam (the steam suggestion was put forth by a German cartoonist). These powered vehicles became known as velocipedes, which can be loosely translated as "speedy feet."

The very first official motorcycle was built by a fellow by the name of Gottlieb Daimler. Here it is, complete with training wheels, circa 1885. *Daimler-Benz Archives*

This standard bicycle has an engine kit installed. The kits were the forerunners to motorized bicycles. This one was built by the du Pont brothers (see chapter 11 for more details on them). *Roy Query Photo, courtesy of the du Pont family*

Although a Frenchman applied for a patent on a steam-powered velocipede in 1868, the first such vehicle to be constructed may have been built in America by Sylvester H. Roper, who definitely built the machine, but whether he did it before or after 1868 is not resolved. In 1879, an Italian patented a "gas-engined velocipede," but there are no records indicating it ran. In 1884, one Lucius D. Copeland of Philidelphia is known to have put a steam engine on a bicycle.

The next historical quirk is that none of these machines were called motorcycles. The name hadn't been invented or assigned yet, like many of the myriad of new contraptions appearing at that time.

Hold that quirk, while we return to the bicycle's evolution. The oval track racers decided it would be fair to speed things up by decreasing air resistance. They did that by building a machine powered by a single-cylinder engine that pushed a windshield around the track. The bicyclist pedaled along behind the shield, suddenly able to pedal to considerably higher speeds. These big, clumsy machines were built in France, mostly because the French were technical leaders at that time.

These pacers followed Daimler's machine. Others built similar units, and the road-going production motorcycle arrived in 1895, from a company called Hildrebrand and Wulfmiller.

The actual name, motoryycle, just sort of appeared, much like the term "Jeep" and "OK." There are several convincing accounts, none of which have been proven beyond doubt.

By 1900, the motorcycle as we know it today had been invented, in the sense that it now had two wheels, an engine in between them, and a rider perched above the engine. U.S. firms were combining their brand of bicycle with French engines, and youth and mechanical magazines of the day advertised plans and kits for powering your bicycle at home—more about this thirty years later in this account.

The Dynamic Duo

When the right people have the right idea at the right time, they make history. Indian's history begins with two men who were perfectly matched: they shared a common enthusiasm and their talents were complementary. (Note: Indian comes first here because Indian arrived first, and as you will see, Indian was ahead of Harley in most ways for most of their rivalry.)

The older half of the duo was George Hendee. He was born into a prosperous family in Watertown, Connecticut, then a thriving manufacturing town. When Hendee was still in high school he began racing bicycles, the penny-farthing high wheelers. He was very good. He won the national mile, two mile, five mile, ten mile, and twenty-mile championships, and his biographer, J.J. O'Conner, head of Indian's publicity department, who admit-

tedly worked for the company at the time and had reason to make the founder look good, calculated that during his career, Hendee had entered 309 match races and won 302 of them. Hendee raced as an amateur, taking no money even when he ran against the pros. Americans were more conscious of class then, as proven by the same biographer, who noted that Hendee "never turned 'pro' himself, preserving his *clean* (emphasis added) standing to the day of his retirement."

When Hendee retired from racing, he enrolled in the College of the Free Market, that is, he became a sales rep., then a dealer in bicycles, then a partner in a factory, and finally owned the whole thing. He named the company the Hendee Manufacturing Company, and the bicycles were branded with "Silver King."

The second half of the duo was Oscar Hedstrom, who was born in Sweden and came to the United States as a youth. He was also a bicycle enthusiast, a skilled rider, a machinist, and a thinker. He went into business building racing bikes. When the French pacers arrived, Hedstrom noticed how sloppy they were and thought, I can do better than that. Working on his own, Hedstrom came up with an improved frame and engine, which would start the first time and run twenty miles, no problem.

Meanwhile, Hendee hadn't lost interest in racing and had in fact become a promoter in Springfield, Massachusetts. He heard about Hedstrom's pacer and invited the self-taught engineer to Springfield where the two hit it off and agreed that the world needed a bicycle you didn't have to pedal.

They became partners, Hedstrom at the drafting table and lathe, Hendee handling the business and the public. At Hendee's request, or perhaps direction, Hedstrom retired from racing and moved into a shop in Middletown, Connecticut. His assignment: design and build the best motorized bicycle that can be made.

Another historical delight: Not long after Daimler's devices became the wave of the future, there was a debate over exactly what the four-wheeled contraptions should be called. "Motorcars," said the English speakers; "Automobiles," countered the French. A public debate followed and lots of names were coined. Americans used both automobile and car, the French stuck with the former, and the English the latter. Hendee liked the name motocycle, with no "r." So, for the next forty years at least, the proper name was Indian Motocycle.

But that came later. Early in 1901 Hedstrom invited Hendee to see what he had built, and it was just what Hendee had ordered. It had a conventional bicycle frame, wheels mounted rigidly in forks, and rear frame members. It had a single cylinder engine where a bicycle's rear frame downtube would be. The engine was just above the sprocket and pedals. The drive was solid, with no clutch or belt between the engine and the rear wheel. It had a coaster brake in the rear hub.

The engine displaced 13 cubic inches and used a mechanical exhaust valve and atmospheric intake with a valve that pulled open when the piston went down and popped shut when the piston came back up. Hedstrom built his own carburetor and muffler. Ignition was by batteries and coil housed in cylinders on the front of the frame.

There was at least one marked advance: a carburetor with provision for speed control. At that stage of engine development, lots of designers felt it was enough to get the fuel and air mixed at all, and they controlled speed with the ignition kill button, a practice that would continue in aircraft until World War I.

All the controls were by rod, bell crank, and lever, and it wasn't easy to route the rods and swivels so the motion of the hand on the lever on the bar was delivered to the carb or ignition. Something would soon be done about that. Most importantly, the prototype was a bicycle with an engine, and it worked.

Hendee and Hedstrom did their own tests, in secret, generations before real rocket scientists tested in places called Skunk Works. Then, Hendee being well ahead of his time in several ways, they called a press conference. There was a famously steep and challenging hill in Springfield, and Hendee persuaded the newspaper guys to come out and watch Hedstrom turn the mountain into a molehill. Hedstrom rode the machine from the shop, and it scooted up the grade so easily he'd slow and stop and start again, just to drive the point home. In June 1901, the public looked at the photos and read the raves. The Indian Motocycle was in business.

The Four Founders

At about the same time, the turn of the century, boyhood pals William Harley and Arthur Davidson had jobs in a fabrication shop in Milwaukee, Wisconsin. Harley, who had gone to work at fifteen in a bicycle shop, was an apprentice draftsman. Davidson was a pattern maker. Neither was more than a casual bicycle enthusiast. They liked machinery, and they liked going places and doing things outdoors, fishing and hunting and so forth.

Company folklore says they began fiddling with engines after hours, perhaps thinking of outboard motors as much a motorized bicycles. (One of their peers at that time was Ole Evinrude, who of course would go on to develop the outboard motor.) In the fall of 1900, the pair began assembling and producing parts for an engine to power a two-wheeler. An older man in the shop had some knowledge of the de Dion engines from France so they followed that general design. Their carburetor was pretty much a fixed setting, not incidentally, with engine speed controlled more by advancing and retarding the spark.

Arthur's older brother, William, was getting married, the legend continues, and when a third brother

Walter, a machinist, came home for the wedding, he was invited to ride the new machine, the joke being that it was in pieces at the time and the other guys hoped he'd put it together, which he did. This was part-time fun, not even up to the status of a hobby. They got an engine that would run, and learned it was too much for the bicycle frame and parts. They reengineered the bicycle with a larger and stronger frame and then expanded the engine as well. They didn't finish the first or second prototypes until 1903, and the three working partners—William didn't get involved until the partners incorporated in 1907—kept their day jobs.

This was very much a family operation. The Davidsons' dad built them a shed, a building so small that when the railroad said the building was in their right-of-way, a bunch of guys from the neighborhood picked the factory up and moved it.

When they went into production, it was with the financial help of a well-to-do uncle. Janet, one of the Davidson sisters, applied red pinstripes to the black paint of the first Harley-Davidson and devised the Harley-Davidson shield that by now is as recognizable as the internationally known logos of Coca-Cola and Ford.

As you can see, Harley-Davidson and Indian began with similarities and differences. Both sets of entrepreneurs were vigorous, intelligent, and ambitious. They came from solid and successful backgrounds. Hendee's was the most prosperous; witness his ability to race for fun for several years. The others were, to coin a phrase, starched blue collar class. They had valuable skills, and they knew it. They weren't afraid of taking chances or betting on themselves. Hendee and Hedstrom were older when the story begins and they had more experience in business and probably in life as well. Indian began as an addition to a product line, from a firm with factory and dealerships, with experienced management. Harley-Davidson had more to learn.

Indian had an engineering genius and a born promoter. When it became clear that motorcycles could be a business, William Harley quit the shop and enrolled in college, to become the engineer the four knew would be needed, while the Davidsons ran the shop and went on the road. (Harley's name comes first, by the way, because it sounds better than Davidson-Harley, despite the fact that the Davidsons outnumbered Harley three to one.)

What seems to be the major factor, though, was that these two partnerships were the right mix of talents at the perfect time. As they needed to be.

*O*ne of Indian's founding fathers, Oscar Hedstrom, was inspired to build this circa 1901 prototype by the French-built bicycle racing pace vehicles. *Don Emde*

Chapter Two

First Machines

Two Among Many

One of motorcycling history's amazing facts is that from late in the nineteenth century until late in the twentieth, there were several hundred brands of motorcycles offered in the American market, with names stretching all the way from Ace to Zimmerman. When glances becomes serious research, though, the long list turns out to be both more and less than the full story. Indian's early history is the perfect illustration.

George Hendee was an established bicycle maker and Oscar Hedstrom was a proven designer when they went into the motorcycle business. They easily raised the money to expand—something that eventually hurt rather than helped the company as you'll see—but the Indian bicycle plant didn't have a foundry or the equipment to make engines.

Meanwhile, the Aurora Automatic Machinery Company did have such equipment and a foundry. Aurora was getting into the motorcycle business under the brand name Thor, but it wasn't quite sure how to design an engine. The playing field was small enough for the players to know each other, plus Hedstrom's exploits at the Springfield press conference had been highly publicized, as Hendee knew they'd be. So Indian and Aurora did the natural deal, with Aurora making the engines for Indian and getting permission to use Hedstrom's improvements.

Meanwhile, the company making Pope automobiles and bicycles arranged to use Thor engines for the Pope motorcycle, and the holding company had a distribution system for bicycles that was expanded into motorcycles bearing the badges Columbia, Cleveland, and Tribune in the east, and Rambler, Monarch, Imperial, and Crescent in the west.

These machines were not Indians. Unlike Ford and Mercury or Plymouth and Dodge, all the brands used other off-the-shelf parts, as in brakes and wheels and so forth. But the motorcycles were similar in specifications and in the fact that most of those several hundred brands lasted a couple of years or even a couple of examples. If there's a lasting lesson here it's that all the other pioneers paid well-deserved tribute to Hendee and Hedstrom.

Next, there were some early exotics, like the Belgian four-cylinder FN or the fantastic V-8 built by Glenn Curtiss and clocked in 1907 at 137 miles per hour, but the vast majority of those early makers created motorized bicycles, with pedals and coaster brakes and an engine that stopped and started when the pedaler did.

By 1906, as an educated guess, the Indian was still a powered bicycle, the engine still permanently joined to the rear wheel, but the front wheel was suspended: there's a pivot halfway up the fork legs, and the canister above the fender houses a coil spring. *Roy Query photo, courtesy of the du Pont family*

The official 1901 Indian is very little changed from Hedstrom's original; it didn't need much change. Note that it's a bicycle, with pedals and sprocket centered, as if the rider works and the engine helps. *Don Emde*

Early Indian Production

Indian's founders were clearly in step with the majority, while being a couple of football fields ahead of the average motorized bicycles. In 1901, the first year of actual production Indians, they made three examples. One went with Hedstrom on a tour of the bicycle racing stadiums, at which he created a sensation. Another went to England, where it was demonstrated with equal success. And another went to a customer, surely creating demand in its own way.

Sales for 1902 totaled 143, and they multiplied again the next year and again in the year after that. Hedstrom had a policy of improving the machine as ideas occurred to him, but the basic design, the safety bicycle with an engine in place of the rear frame tube, lasted through 1904.

The machine weighed about 98 pounds, the 13-cubic-inch engine delivered a horsepower plus maybe a fraction on a good day, top speed was 25 miles per hour, wheelbase was 48 inches, and you could have any color you wanted, provided that color was dark blue (a slogan credited to, but never uttered by, Henry Ford, by the way). Drive was all chain, primary to the central sprocket and secondary to the rear wheel, which contained the coaster brake, and drive was permanently engaged.

The main control was the valve lifter, which opened the exhaust valve, released compression, and stopped the engine. There were levers for that, for spark timing, and for a basic throttle, although the spark setting did more to control speed than the carb did.

In 1905, the front forks got a coil spring and pivot to allow an inch or so of wheel travel under duress. The levers were replaced by twist grips, working rods, and pivots. In 1906 they experimented with primary drive by gear, requiring the engine to revolve in the other direction.

In that same year Hedstrom came up with a V-twin. The concept wasn't original with him, but he did his usual improvements, with the front cylinder 42 degrees to the original, and the pair still set in the diamond frame. The single cylinder engine was enlarged, to 17.6 cubic inches and 2.25 rated horsepower, and sales kept on growing: 1,181 in 1906, then 2,176 the year after that. Indian was well on its way to becoming the world's largest motorcycle maker.

The Silent Gray Fellow

And what of the rivals? They weren't rivals yet. It's probable that William Harley and Arthur Davidson read about Indian in the enthusiast press. More important, their prototypes didn't hold up under the beating of Wisconsin's highways, presumably worse than those in Connecticut or Massachusetts.

So they designed their final prototype, if that's the word, to be more than a powered bicycle. First, it was larger, with bigger frame tubes and related parts. Next, the engine was bored and stroked to 25 cubic inches with the corresponding increased power and torque. The engine was the same basic de Dion concept, with the intake valve pulled open on the intake stroke and closed by compression, with a cam lobe for the exhaust, and with both valves in a pocket next to the piston.

Next, the safety bicycle had a diamond frame, and when Indian and the others added engines, they did so within the frame, with pedal power central in the layout. Harley and Davidson used a loop frame, with the lower frame tube curled around a central engine and with the pedals set aft. And from the first, the Harley-Davidson had a clutch. It was a rather crude device, intended simply to tighten the drive belt on its engine and rear wheel pulleys, but William Harley wasn't willing to use all chains until he'd worked out a true clutch, which came a few years later. With the other Davidsons joining as their circumstances permitted, and with William Harley corresponding and adding ideas as he picked them up at college, Harley-Davidson was in business.

The first two production motorcycles were sold to people who'd heard of the project and been so impressed by the prototype that they paid half the purchase price up front so the partners could pay the help and buy the raw material and outside bits like tires and batteries. The first official model year was

The first production Harley-Davidsons were more than bicycles plus motors. The pedals are auxiliary and the loop frame was designed for an engine from the beginning. Not only that, the belt drive with tensioner means the engine can run when the machine itself has stopped. © *Harley-Davidson Motor Company*

The early production single needed careful routing of the rods, levers, and pivots from the grips to the carburetor and ignition. And this example, for reasons not in the records, has a gear primary joining the engine sprocket to the pedaled sprocket. All the others are chain drive, meaning the engine in this Indian has to run in a reverse direction from usual. *Roy Query photo, courtesy of the du Pont family*

*H*ere's an odd one. The men who own and restored this pioneer say it was made by a guy named Franklin, and that it was made in 1899, predating Hedstrom's work. Collectors and restorers who don't have a stake in this say it's one of the Aurora-based machines, with Hedstrom's design being used under license. The frame is clearly different from the early Indians, but the best bet has to be that Franklin bought the parts or modified an early Indian.

*V*ery early Indian V-twin shows how easily the second cylinder fitted onto the crankcase and into the bicycle frame of the single. The plunger aft and outboard of the rear cylinder is an oiler for the chain.

*T*he new intake camshaft and the housing for the ignition drive are attached outside of the crankcase proper. Natural rubber is white, by the way, and tires didn't get black until the rubber was mixed with carbon black, for durability.

1904. Like the other manufacturers, Harley-Davidson made running changes and expanded as it could, purchasing land and constructing a real factory, to be enlarged as the need arose.

The partners had always considered the motorcycle to be a useful helper, so they fitted an effective muffler to make it quiet. When they changed the paint from black to gray, they called the lone model in the catalog the Silent Gray Fellow.

William Harley was experimenting, so in 1907 the front wheel was suspended, with a leading-link, two pairs of parallel struts, and some coil springs, a design that would remain a Harley feature for nearly 40 years and would be revived 30 years after that, when the company discovered that the best (only?) way to move forward was to look back.

Hints of Things to Come

When J. J. O'Conner, the larger-than-life sales manager for Indian during its later boom years, wrote up his version of the pioneer days, he felt it worth mentioning that even then, when every motor trip was an adventure if not a gamble, class warfare had already begun.

"The early auto owners did not like their motorcycling brothers because we could pass their expensive cars on the road and we also seemed able to fix our machines when they quit, which was more than the average fellow behind a steering wheel could do."

Interesting. When Marlon Brando starred in *The Wild Ones* and *Life* magazine staged the photo of the drunken biker, they weren't inventing a prejudice, they were catering to one. And in doing so, the car people motivated the motorcyclists into thinking socially.

Another indication of things to come occurred when Hendee and Hedstrom expanded their business, which they did with the help of investors. When Harley and the Davidsons expanded, they relied on family for labor, loans, and advice. These different financial tactics are indicative of the different positions in life occupied by the six founders: they were at the opposite edges of their generation. Hendee was the oldest, born in 1866, while Arthur Davidson, the youngest, was born in 1881. Indian's owners already had business experience when they founded their firm, whereas Harley-Davidson was four young men with experience in work but not

Harley-Davidson's first production machines were obviously based on the prototype, with the pedals as accessories and the engine centered in the loop frame. One major change was the leading-link front suspension. The early H-D single was known as the Silent Gray Fellow because it was, well, gray and silent. Roy Kidney/Vintage Museum

The 1912 single had one speed, but there were several options. This example is the basic version, with belt drive and a tensioner and magneto ignition (behind the cylinder). For another 10 dollars, you could get a rear hub that contained a clutch and there options for headlight and colors other than red to go with the Renault gray shown here. Roy Kidney/Vintage Museum

in management. They were entrepreneurs with more to learn and more aware, the record hints, of what they didn't know.

You guessed right: we're going to lean heavily on hindsight. But that's fair, because just as we never know we've been in a golden age until it's over, so do eras conclude while we're looking at something else.

The historical consensus at this writing is that by 1908 the motorcycle had replaced the motor-powered bicycle. The pedal bike with power assist was charming. There was an innocent pleasure in ambling down leafy lanes at 20 per, and those of us who never did it sometimes wish we had. But those who were there voted by resting their feet. By 1908, the issue was settled. The powered bicycle had improved itself out of the picture. There would still be kit engines for real bicycles, and later there would be mopeds, but in the main, from 1908 on, the motorcycle would rule.

Chapter Three

The Hendee Special

Two Leaps Too Far

It's easy to declare an idea or a product ahead of its time, but making the case can be tough. If, for example, the man who came up with *TV Guide* had done so before the other man invented the picture tube that became television, he would clearly have been ahead of his time. For a less obvious situation, consider this Indian press release from 1914:

"Only the engineering staff which conceived and executed the motorcycle sensation of 1913—the Cradle Spring Frame—could add to that triumph in 1914 a practical electric system for motorcycle use. They waited only long enough to allow the electric starter and electric lighting to prove themselves on the automobile. Then they undertook the exhaustive work of experimenting, testing, discarding, selecting, and evolving Motorcycle Electricity, which has its final and perfected form in the 1914 Indian."

Oh my. Indian had arrived at both its best of times and its worst of times. For the best part, we move back several years. Hedstrom was working hard and well. Indian added a V-twin model to the line, adopted mechanical intake valves, a clutch, a two-speed gearbox, cables for the twist controls, and an improved front suspension with auto-style leaf spring. The bicycle-style diamond frame was replaced by the loop frame, as seen on Harleys, and

the engine was moved to the center of the vee instead of being part of the frame's downtube.

Indian had more racing wins than can be listed (see the next chapter for the highlights), and racers could buy competition models direct, priced to sell. The range of models and the excellence of the designs made Indian the largest motorcycle maker in the world, with outlets around the globe.

But Hedstrom wanted to make the machines even better, and while Hendee knew the improved product meant improved sales, he was also aware that the mass-produced car, with top and side curtains and all the comforts you could carry, was reducing the motorcycle's practical appeal.

So with Hendee's approval, Hedstrom designed a rear suspension for the top-of-the-line V-twin. It was a remarkable job. The description reads like 1973 instead of 1913, with a swingarm pivoting off the rear of the frame, controlled by a pair of springs, and offering a full five inches of wheel travel.

It probably wasn't the very first suspension, the need for which was as sharp and clear as the jolts dealt by the primitive roads of the time, but it was new and was as good at it could be, for the money and with the materials at hand. Hendee knew marketing. Suspension was a standard item in 1913, but became an option for

The Hendee Special, consisting of the leaf-spring front suspension, the new-for-1913 leaf spring with swingarm rear suspension, and the classic Hedstrom-style intake-over-exhaust V-twin. *Cycle World*

The round housing at the engine's left front is a combination electric starter and generator; flip the switch to choose the function. The box beneath the seat houses the batteries, which were big enough but not strong enough for the job. *Cycle World*

The daring young man on his Indian twin is Hap Alzina, who will figure large in this history, and the passenger is wife-to-be Lil. He's got floorboards for his feet, she has lots of courage, and the Indian has the classic leaf-spring front suspension and a kick starter, in front of Hap's boot. *Hap Alzina Archives*

1914 and later. The buyer who needed to save money and thus justify his motorcycle could do without.

Hedstrom was also at work on the electric starter. Pedal starts and running starts had been replaced by what H-D elegantly named the step-starter, so much nicer than pedalling the engine into life. When the car companies followed Boss Kettering's trail and added self-starting to autos, they more than doubled their potential buying public, as there must have been men who weren't any happier about breaking their arms with the ol' hand crank than women were.

Later accounts said that Hendee urged the development of the electric starter, and Hedstrom wasn't sure it was as easy as it looked. They hired an electrical firm to help, and Hedstrom laid out a system whereby an electric motor was connected to the crankshaft with a chain. Set a switch one way and the pair of batteries powered the electric motor and spun the engine. When it fired up, you threw the switch and the spinning engine transformed the motor into a generator and did the chemical number on the batteries.

The idea was a good one and the execution so deft that some history books have said that the model didn't have a generator at all.

The Technology Gap

The fatal flaws in both the rear suspension and the electric starter didn't come from the drawing board. Historian Griff Borgeson, whose overall knowledge of this era is unequaled, writes that before World War I the United States was still a "wild, woolly, and provincial country."

We may have had Yankee ingenuity, he says, but until the pressure of war forced industry and government to spend for research, we were short on some sciences. The better car makers bragged (until the war, obviously) that they used Krupp steel from Germany, and they had their crankshafts and crankcases forged and cast in France because it couldn't be done that well (yet) here.

As a result, when the suspended Indians with that perfected electrical system hit the streets, the

linkage on the springs, links, and swingarm wore, got loose, the bike wobbled, and the drive chains jumped the track. The starter/generator worked and the batteries held up . . . in the lab. But the streets were mean, the riders didn't maintain the devices, and the batteries broke and ran down. The owners reacted about how you'd expect: with complaints, threats, and imprecations. The electrically perfected Hendee Specials were recalled and stripped of the systems, fitted with kick start, and returned to their owners with money and apologies. The debacle cost the company money and dealt a tremendous blow to Indian's prestige. The biggest and the best had taken motorcycling's major pratfall.

And naturally, Harley-Davidson, where the kick start would remain king for the next 40 years, didn't mind telling potential buyers and Indian owners just how badly the experiment had gone, while adding that the rear suspension was unsound and that rigidly mounted rear wheels didn't throw chains.

Motorcycling had become a social sport by the teens, witness this gathering—all Harley-Davidsons, near as we can tell—before embarking on a Sunday ride. © Harley-Davidson Motor Company

25

An Incredible Journey

Ever notice how a good story is better when you don't know all the details and wish you did?

Seen here is a 1914 Hendee Special. When the model was declared a disaster, Indian recalled them all and destroyed, or so they thought, all the evidence. For years even Indian collectors thought all the Specials were gone for good.

What nobody knew was that in the Midwest, in 1914, a hardware store clerk wanted one but couldn't pay for it. His kind boss offered to buy one for him and put it in the basement until the young man had saved the money. Forty years later, when the owner died and they tore down the hardware store, there in the basement was the motorcycle you see here. Just as you see it here. With ten miles on the odometer.

What happened to the young man? Nobody knows. The romantic guess is that he was killed in action, but it's just as likely that the next spring his fancy turned to girls and she said, "No noisy contraptions," and that was that. What counts now is that the current owner, who did not wish to be identified, displays this treasure at shows. It now has 100 miles on the clock, and the electric starter works.

What did they do when they got there, on those Sunday rides? Had fun. Lil Alzina took this photo, presumably of husband Hap in the white shirt facing off with a guy on a Harley V-twin, at Golden Gate Park in San Francisco, 1918. It has to be some form of bump-start contest. *Hap Alzina Archives*

The suspension would remain on Indians for the next several years, not incidentally, but would be discarded and ignored by Harley and Indian for the next 40 years.

Now, the really bad part: remember that Hendee and Hedstrom had investors; and the guys who'd put up the money for the plant and the expansions had done it for the money. They didn't see why Hendee and Hedstrom had to keep spending more money on the product. And they said so, often enough that the founders got tired of hearing about it. Hendee and Hedstrom, who had both made their fortunes and bought country estates in Massachusetts and Connecticut respectively, decided to sell their interest in Indian and become country squires.

Note here that they weren't kicked out, nor was this a hostile takeover, nor were the new owners bad guys, nor did Indian cease producing excellent products.

This retirement of the founders wasn't a classic horror story. Call it a subtle tragedy. The electric leg model was named the Hendee Special in tribute to the man. But when things went wrong, he wasn't there to defend the project. And Hedstrom wasn't there to fix it. Given time and the technical know-how that came from the war, Hedstrom and Hendee could have turned the Hendee Special into a success, and history would be different. Which is as easy to say as the business about being ahead of its time.

Meanwhile, several dozen motorcycle makers were still in business, with Harley-Davidson the

*H*ap Alzina again, at the top of Mt. Tamalpais, Marin County, California, 1915. He's ridden his Indian three-speed to the peak via railroad tracks, no kidding, to get publicity for U.S. Tire, whose shirt he's wearing.

*Y*es, these are women, who in 1914 are riding their Harley with sidecar from, as the sign says, Washington, Pa. to Tulsa, OK. Not only that, the woman on the right has a shirt with the H-D shield, generations before such became fashionable. The lady in the background has to be saying, Gosh, I didn't know women rode motorcycles and yes, to be fair, if it hadn't been news they wouldn't have been in the photo, eh? Point here is, women have been riding since riding began. © *Harley-Davidson Motor Company*

𝒯remendous progress has been made with this 1913 Indian twin. There is suspension front and rear, there's a clutch and a gearbox, and the engine is in the center of the frame with the pedals aft. *Roy Kidney/Vintage Museum*

leading contender but not the only one, and you can bet they all took lots of notes. Harley's engineering records show there was some sort of V-twin experiment in 1907, of which no details have yet been found but which was perhaps inspired by the Indian V-twin introduced in 1906.

The first production Harley V-twin, the Model 5D, with an included angle of 45 degrees as opposed to Indian's 42 degrees, came out in 1909. And went right back. The engine still had

atmospheric intake valves and was nearly impossible to start. In 1911, the engine returned, this time with camshaft activation for intake and exhaust, and Harley has made V-twins ever since. The tensioned drive belts were replaced with a clutch and three-speed gearbox. A generator, lights, and "electric signal" were options (the electric signal was a horn, except that back when people cared about their language, it wasn't called a horn if it didn't have a bell and tube).

Just as Indian's new managers weren't villains, so weren't Harley's original owners stuck in the mud. They were more cautious, and they were willing to learn from the problems of the other guys. And—another little item we'll meet again—when Indian went to rear suspension, Harley used a seat on a suspended post. The rider was suspended, you could say. It worked, the ride was comfortable, and nothing went wrong.

The moral was that Indian lost a major battle. But so did innovation.

When Talk Wasn't Cheap

Before we had e-mail, voice mail, work stations, or truly efficient telephone service, there was the telegram. And there was a charge, usually so much per word. But as always, where there are charges, there are ways around them. In 1915 a copy of Indian Motocycle Company's telegraph code was sent to all the dealers, noting "The use of this code . . . will effect a considerable saving in telegram charges. In wiring the factory use the code wherever possible."

The Cradle Spring model was usable transportation, with headlight, tiny taillight—traffic wasn't a problem in those days—and even a leather case for tools. The 1913 Indian twin was the most advanced motorcycle in the world. *Roy Kidney/Vintage Museum*

Father and son at the races is the obvious guess. The bike is a Powerplus in racing trim, and the caps make you wish sons still dressed like dads. Hap Alzina Archives

Why Big Daddy has ridden his intake-over-exhaust V-twin into the surf has been lost in time but the girl's reaction—Oh Dad!, as only a daughter can deliver it—will be familiar to all dads and daughters. Hap Alzina Archives

Then came: (this is a sample of the 46 code words)

BALK   Model E-3, Single-Cylinder Three-Speed Service
ELAPSE   Gear for hilly country
GET   Answer by wire
GOOD   Have you shipped?
KIT   Shipment delayed on account of __

And so it went. What the dealer did was sent the telegram, maybe Good Balk Get, and the factory would reply Head Hide Hot (Was shipped by freight, Have written you today, We are sending tracer), and the message was sent at minimum cost. What AT&T thought of this isn't in the archives.

Some Words from the Sponsors

Once the motorcycle became a reliable transportation machine, the advertisements focused on that achievement. For instance, the 1913 Indians were extolled as efficient and easily maintained, as proven by the police departments. At the same time Pierce's advertisers claimed that it would ". . . last longer and give better service under all road conditions than any other motorcycle." Or, to give another example: "All roads are smooth to the Flying Merkel."

There was hype to make even a TV evangelist blush: The 1912 Iver-Johnson was extolled to be " a motorcycle which has been pronounced by impartial experts to be the finest example of mechanical design and construction ever produced in a motor driven vehicle." The same company also offered "an absolutely perfect" bicycle and revolvers that were "accurate and hard-hitting." Imagine saying that on the salespitch channel.

Early Harley-Davidson ads offered an intriguing blend of virtues. In 1911 an ad asked "A warm noon lunch at home or a cold bite downtown? A short run home in the open or an hour in a stuffy [street] car? The cost of operating a Harley-Davidson is very low . . . less than any other mode of transportation. The Harley-Davidson is a clean motorcycle and can be ridden without damage to your 'best clothes,' runs as quietly as a high-priced automobile or with a sharp warning 'pop' at the rider's option."

Just wait 'til they come up with "Loud Pipes Save Lives."

Speaking of off-road machines, these guys were loaded for, OK, deer not bear, and it paid off. Passenger seats were very separate then. Judging from the expressions on the faces of the guys on the solo and the guys with the chair, both bucks fell victim to the latter team.
© *Harley-Davidson Motor Company*

Alfred LeRoy didn't let physical problems interfere with his riding. His 1916 J-series Harley twin had a sidecar and remote controls for him, and the sidecar has a sidecar for his dog.
© *Harley-Davidson Motor Company*

*I*rving F. Brown and his Harley J,
ready for the open road of 1914.
© *Harley-Davidson Motor Company*

*E*verybody knew the police had to get there quickly and
reliably, so if the police used Indians, as the ad proves they
did, why then Indians had to be practical and reliable.

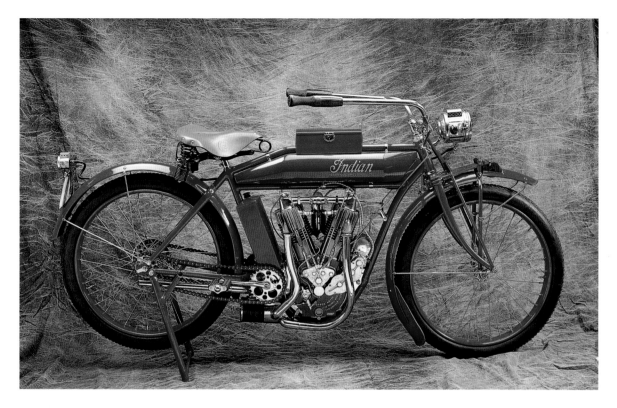

By 1912, motorcycles were becoming more than just motor-powered bicycles; witness this 1912 Indian twin with the engine centered and the pedals secondary. *Jeff Hackett*

The clutch had been incorporated into the drive sprocket by 1912, but starting still meant pedaling because the Indian kick start didn't arrive until the next year. *Jeff Hackett*

Chapter Four

Racing, Part I

On Track at Last

When Jim Davis was 12 years old, back in 1908, he decided he'd like to have a motorcycle. So he asked his dad for one, and his dad got him a sporting Yale, one of the best and the fastest. Just like that. Things must have been different then.

As it happens, dad did the right thing. By 1916 Davis was on the Indian factory team. This was in the days of brakeless racing machines that ran locked in gear with the throttle wide open, on banked board speedways that allowed lap speeds of 120 miles per hour. Jim Davis clearly was a man of skill and bravery. Not to mention nerve.

Early in 1920, Davis recalled 75 years later, "I went to Phoenix with two bikes. The referee said I couldn't ride, that there was a new rule and they'd already picked the riders." Professional racing at the time was controlled by a trade group, heavily backed by the major manufacturers and deeply political. Davis knew this.

"I said, 'If A. B. Coffman [head honcho of the sanctioning body] says I can ride, can I ride?' They said yes, if they got a telegram. So I went downtown and persuaded the girl to send a telegram saying I could ride and signed by A. B. Coffman. I rode, won the event, and got the money.

"When I got back to Los Angeles the referee there, who was a friend of mine, said I couldn't ride. I asked why not and he said he didn't know, but he'd just gotten a letter saying I was suspended for a year. So that's why I left Indian."

Pause while Davis lets the suspense build.

"A week or so later the Harley team manager, Bill Ottoway, asked if I'd like to ride a Harley. I said sure, but I'm suspended. A week later, I was back racing."

How'd that happen?

"The Harley factory did it. They supported the association, and I guess they just put on the pressure."

One of the ways they applied pressure was to get Coffman fired. And that's how it was back then. How'd it get that way? It's fair to say that bicycle racing was father to the motorcycle and that the bicycle was midwife to motorcycle racing. First, the motorized bicycle was treated as a bicycle plus, with the riders and the reporting coming from the bicycle crowd.

Next, those pioneer motorcyclists were bicyclists first.

So it's no surprise that the early motorcycling competion was won by bicycle racers, most notably Hendee, Hedstrom, and friends. An Indian won what seems to have been the first hillclimb, in the Bronx in 1902. Later that year, the founders and an Indian

Later intake-over-exhaust racers were obviously related to the more exotic eight-valvers. This is a 1926 FHAC, with F designating the series and the other letters being the factory's code for Don't Sell These Engines, which they didn't officially do This example is especially rare, with tapered cylinder fins from Ricardo; the factory's cylinders have fins of equal width up and down. Roy Kidney/Daniel Statnekov

Indian raced early, witness this 1908 V-twin with diamond frame and the rear cylinder serving as a frame tube. Note the streamlined fuel tank and the rider's precarious perch. *Jeff Hackett*

Loop frames had swept the board, so to speak, by 1914. This board-track single has centered the engine and the rider and looks much more sturdy in general. *Jeff Hackett*

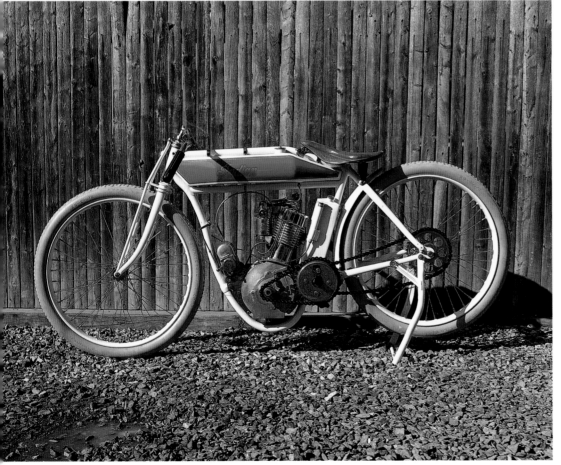

dealer, George Holden, finished one-two-three with perfect scores in the first national endurance run, New York to Boston. The Indian team went gold in the endurance run again in 1903, wth Hendee pausing in Hartford to have his bloodied hands bandaged, then heading for the finish. Too heroic to be true? "I was there," O'Conner later wrote, "I saw it."

Holden is credited with winning the first dirt track race, a venue that the bicyclists didn't use, and Hedstrom rode a souped-up Indian five miles at Ormond Beach, Florida (the track was later moved south to Daytona Beach) in five minutes, 27 seconds. The story O'Conner conveniently left out is that Hedstrom lost a match race to the Winton Bullet, the fastest car on the beach at that time.

In 1908, Indian added racing models—V-twins and singles stripped of road equipment—to their line. And one of the rivalry's traditions began way back then, when Walter Davidson rode a Silent Gray Fellow to first place in 1908 and achieved a perfect score in the Federation of American Motorcyclists' national endurance run.

The subplot here is that Harley-Davidson wasn't a racing company. They believed in the sport, and Walter Davidson and William Harley were gifted rid-

ers, but they weren't racers at heart and diverting money from research, expansion, better material, or whatever into something as intangible as a professional racing team didn't make the sort of careful sense H-D's founders were becoming famous for.

Which is not to say Indian had the field to itself. When 100 brands were on the market, a dozen of them raced. When there were a dozen healthy factories, they backed six teams.

Motorcycle racing became more than a sport. The reliability runs became point-to-point races such as San Diego to Phoenix, which was a route that didn't even have a road. There were races on horse tracks and on banked board tracks, those incredible speeds and crowds to match.

Hedstrom and staff, notably a self-taught designer named Charles Gustafson and an Irish-born racer and engineer named Charles Franklin, were

*O*ne reason the singles tilted back was so the same cases could be used for twins. The rigid front wheel is braced with struts and there are no brakes. *Jeff Hackett*

*J*im Davis, during his second stint on the Indian factory team, aboard his 61-cubic-inch twin at Altoona, Pennsylvania. The front spring has been taped to keep out dust, and the forks are fitted with a damper. Two carburetors were being used even way back then. *Hap Alzina Archives*

more examples than will fit this space, rode an eight-valve for 300 miles in less than 300 minutes and set world records for two, four, five, and six hours. Earlier, the intake-over-exhaust version had won the Isle of Man TT.

Later versions, done by Franklin or Gustafson, reverted to closer to stock, as in smaller cases, with even more power. This was almost a happy accident because the original reason for the multiple valves was that metallurgy was behind the times and valves broke. But small ones didn't break as often as larger ones, so four small was safer than two large, which had ramifications later. More important at the time, Indian listed the racing engines in the catalog and sold them to the public.

The Rivalry Begins

H-D's founders didn't leave us the notes of their debate and change of heart regarding racing, but on July 4, 1914, six top riders entered the Dodge City, Kansas, 300-mile road race, riding the pocket-valve V-twin modified Harleys. The factory support was under the table, the bikes weren't up to the job, and the only two running at the finish were well off the pace. But the best machine had been in a duel for the lead at one point. William Harley and Walter Davidson had been in the crowd, and we don't need notes to know that they'd made up their minds.

In November 1914, the factory came into the open for the 300-mile road race national at Savannah, Georgia. (Road race meant dirt roads, by the way, with turns in both directions. And if it took six or more hours to run a 300-mile race, nobody cared, not in the days of all-day sermons and political speeches.)

A Harley finished third, behind an Indian and an Excelsior. At that point the two latter makes had made up most of the fields, supplemented by the fast-but-quirky overhead cam Cyclone, which was literally more powerful than it could stand. Excelsior was a good machine but didn't have the resources of the other two, which by then were one and two in sales and well beyond whoever was in third.

ready. Spurred by the speed of rival Excelsior, Indian offered racing models topped with overhead valves, four valves per cylinder. This was in 1911, in case anybody thinks the idea is new.

Indian's first racing engines were built using stock cases, but the increased power and stress required larger and beefier cases in later versions, leading to the four-valve "big-base" engines. (Author's note: There's a usage problem here, in that factories often describe the engine with the total number of valves, which impresses but confuses. For example, my Honda 250 single has four valves and so does my Harley twin. The Indian racer had eight valves, as did the four-cylinder Model T Ford. Under protest and because that's how most people speak, we'll refer to the four-per-cylinder twins as eight-valves, OK?)

In 1912, Indian became the world's largest motorcycle maker, it also became the world's fastest motorcycle. Charles Franklin, just to use one of

*H*arley team bike has a production look to it but don't be fooled: the frame, forks, and wheelbase are shorter than the road V-twins of the time. The engine is a full-race intake-over-exhaust 61-cubic-inch unit. Owner Daniel Statnekov and restorer Brad Wilmarth say by the best evidence this machine was a 1916 model but because the racing engines were built on the smaller crankcases not made after 1915, sometimes it's difficult to know the exact age. *Roy Kidney/Daniel Statnekov*

*A*ll the valves are now mechanically operated. The small lever aft of the front exhaust pipe is the valve lifter, which releases compression for starting and stopping the engine. The pedals? Look closely: the pedals are strapped to the frame. They aren't used for starting anymore, but it was easier to fix them in place than to take them off and install some other sort of footpeg.

Teamwork. This is the Indian factory team just after they rode 100 miles in 75 minutes at the Playa del Rey, California, one-mile board track. The seated guys in jerseys are the riders, the men clutching stopwatches are the timers, and the chap with the revolver has to be the starter, or the boss. *Hap Alzina Archives*

Walter Davidson believed in the sport of racing and was, by the record, good at it. He's just established Harley-Davidson's strength and speed by winning an endurance run with a better-than-perfect score. This is 1908 and his production H-D single has the leading-link suspension designed by William Harley in study hall. The controls for spark and throttle are still levers, sited on the right side of the fuel tank. *© Harley-Davidson Motor Company*

Call it Harley vs. Indian. There were some natural parallels. H-D had been offering a special series of pocket-valve V-twins, more carefully matched, balanced, and assembled. These became the basis for the racing 61 cubic-inch twins and 30-50 cubic inches—half a twin—singles. Bill Ottoway, whom we met earlier in his role of political activist, was hired as William Harley's assistant in the engineering department, with a sideline of racing team manager, as seen with Hedstrom and Gustafson at Indian.

Then, in 1916, H-D came out with an eight-valve twin and four-valve single full racers. They were an advance, in that the cylinder head design gained from what the warring nations had learned from airplane engines, and the eight valves were operated by four camshaft lobes instead of two lobes and a complicated system of rockers.

The Harley eight-valve engines were very special. They seem to have been faster than the Indian versions, and while they were listed for sale, the prices were $1,400 for the single and $1,500 for the twin, versus $300 and $350 for the Indians. Obviously Harley didn't want these bikes in the hands of the public.

As it happened, none of the eight-valve engines were officially sold, and the only reason that some still survive is because they were smuggled out or sold for political reasons, which gives us a rare chance to thank politics.

There was a tremendous variety of racing in this first of our sport's Golden Ages, with point-to-point, dirt and flat track, road course, and fairgrounds' ovals, and long and short banked board speedways. Machines evolved to match. They burned gasoline or alcohol, were singles or twins, had overhead valve or intake-over-exhaust, and had clutch and gearbox, or were locked in top gear.

First one team and then the other would assemble four, five, or six of the best men, and the press would happily label that team The Wrecking Crew and disclaim on the rivalry.

For the inside look, we return to Jim Davis. The Indian and H-D teams were remarkably alike. All the riders had the same equipment, and if one man or his mechanic or the boys back at the factory came up with something, every member of the team could use it, "If you wanted it."

"We didn't do much work on the bikes. The factory shipped spare engines, ready to go, with the bikes, and if one went bad, they'd just take it out and put another in the frame. And you know, we didn't have brakes or rear suspension on the track bikes, so there wasn't much else to do."

The team members got salaries, not as much as the stars of today but better than staying home on the farm, and their expenses were paid on the road.

Both Ottoway and Gustafson were intelligent and fair men, Davis recalls, and he never had trouble with either. How about the fans? Did they mind when he switched from Indian to Harley, then back to Indian and then again to Harley?

"Oh no. They had the option to buy or ride what they liked, just as we did."

Well then, why switch?

Policy. Harley-Davidson won everything with the eight-valve engines, so they called them all in, disbanded the team, and left the pros to compete with their intake-over-exhaust machines, which put Davis back in the Indian camp. Then came the Depression, Indian folded its racing tent, and Harley was the only firm making racing engines, so Davis went back to H-D.

They'd say "We're gonna quit racing," and you'd join the other side.

"I didn't care which one I rode, one was as good as the other," Davis said.

Indian riders, note the plural, won every national championship event in 1928 and 1929. Then the tables turned and in 1935, Harley's Joe Petrali, the only member of the sport's only factory team, won every national event, by himself. The only man to come close to Petrali on his Harley was Jim Davis, on an Indian, who out-qualified Petrali at the Syracuse Mile, 44.28 seconds versus 44:30.

So even when it was one-sided, the other side had someone to cheer for.

Jake DeRosier: A Tragedy

One of George Hendee's secret weapons was the ability to spot talent. When he embarked on his

career as a bicycle maker, he was quick to enlist the aid of a young racer named Jacob DeRosier, who quickly became one of the best riders on the circuit. When Hendee expanded into motorcycles, so did DeRosier, who was also a skilled mechanic and thus suited to dealing with the mechanical shortcomings of the day.

DeRosier was one of the team that went 1-2-3 in the first American competitive event. He won on Hedstrom's experimental V-twin in 1906, he set speed records on the bicycle board tracks, and he became a salaried professional racer on the Indian factory team.

*P*roduction-based racing has been with us for a long time; this is an oval-track racer built by modifying an Indian Scout. *Jeff Hackett*

*T*his racer is not all that different from the stock machine. For instance, the direct shifting is done by the rear lever. The vertical control is the valve lifter, which facilitated starts and stops. *Jeff Hackett*

is, Europe, would be surprised if the American Indian wasn't as fast as its claimed records said it was.

Then came an incident for which no explanation has ever sufficed. DeRosier came home from his triumphs overseas and learned that Indian had developed the eight-valve engine, best engine in the sport. Except that there wasn't one for him. Some accounts said Hendee fired DeRosier, no grounds given. Other stories have DeRosier quitting the team in anger, surely justified if it's true that he didn't get one of the new machines. Either way, DeRosier joined the Excelsior team, where he wasn't as good, never mind that his lifetime record was something like 900 races won.

Then came a terrible crash. One of his legs was mangled, and during the series of operations that followed, infection set in. Medicine then was on a par with metallurgy, and DeRosier died.

Hendee ordered five minutes of silence at the Indian plant, and the flag there was flown at half mast. Clearly, Hendee grieved for his former protégé. But he never explained why DeRosier didn't get the eight-valve.

*I*t's 1920, and Harley-Davidson has gone professional. This is Curly Fredericks at the Chicago board track in 1920. The engine is a production-based intake-over-exhaust twin, and the controls have been moved to the handlebars. © *Harley-Davidson Motor Company*

*I*ndian had become the largest motorcycle manufacturer in the world and was racing (and winning) everywhere. Nor did the factory mind telling people about Indian's victories. (The Isle of Man races were England's most important events. After this, they no longer made fun of America's claims to speed). *Cycle World*

In 1909, Indian lured away Reading-Standard's designer, Charles Gustafson, so when motorcycles hit the banked board speedways, the California promoter, Jack Prince, persuaded DeRosier to ride for Indian in a series of match races against Reading-Standard star, Paul Derkum.

DeRosier won every race. He went overseas and won the Isle of Man TT, an effective retort to the English press' remarks about how nobody in the real world, that

1924
Indian
TWIN CYLINDER DAYTONA FRAME
SPEEDWAY RACER
WITH FLXI SIDECAR
EX-STEVE McQUEEN COLLECTION

Moat popular racing sidecars were made by the Flxible Co., and that's how they spelled it. The rider could bank the rig in turns by pushing on it with his right leg. This is a 1924 example. *Jeff Hackett*

Gene Walker, on this eight-valve Indian twin, was the first rider officially to cover a full mile at better than 100 miles per hour, at Daytona Beach in 1920, with official timed runs of 115.79 miles per hour for the full kilometer and 103.70 miles per hour for the full mile. *Cycle World*

This eight-valve Harley-Davidson, circa 1923, shows clear progression from 1916, as in the keystone frame and lower engine, frame, and seat. Leading-link forks are carefully controlled with friction dampers top and bottom. This example was raced by England's legendary Fred Dixon and is one of a handful of surviving eight-valve Harleys. *Roy Kidney/Daniel Statnekov*

Harley's eight-valve engines had a port for each exhaust valve, which is why there are two pipes on each side. Sometimes these engines ran with bared ports, sometimes pipes of various lengths were used to concentrate the power at a specific engine speed. The gadget at the base of the front cylinder is an oiler, and so is the pipe running from the center of the vee to the primary chain. *Roy Kidney/Daniel Statnekov*

*T*he production-based eight-valve Indians, of which this is an example, were based on the production cases, which were smaller than the purely-racing version.

*H*illclimbing became a major spectator draw in the 1920s and the factories had specials for climbs. This one, circa 1924, has a stretched frame and lightweight front forks. *Jeff Hackett*

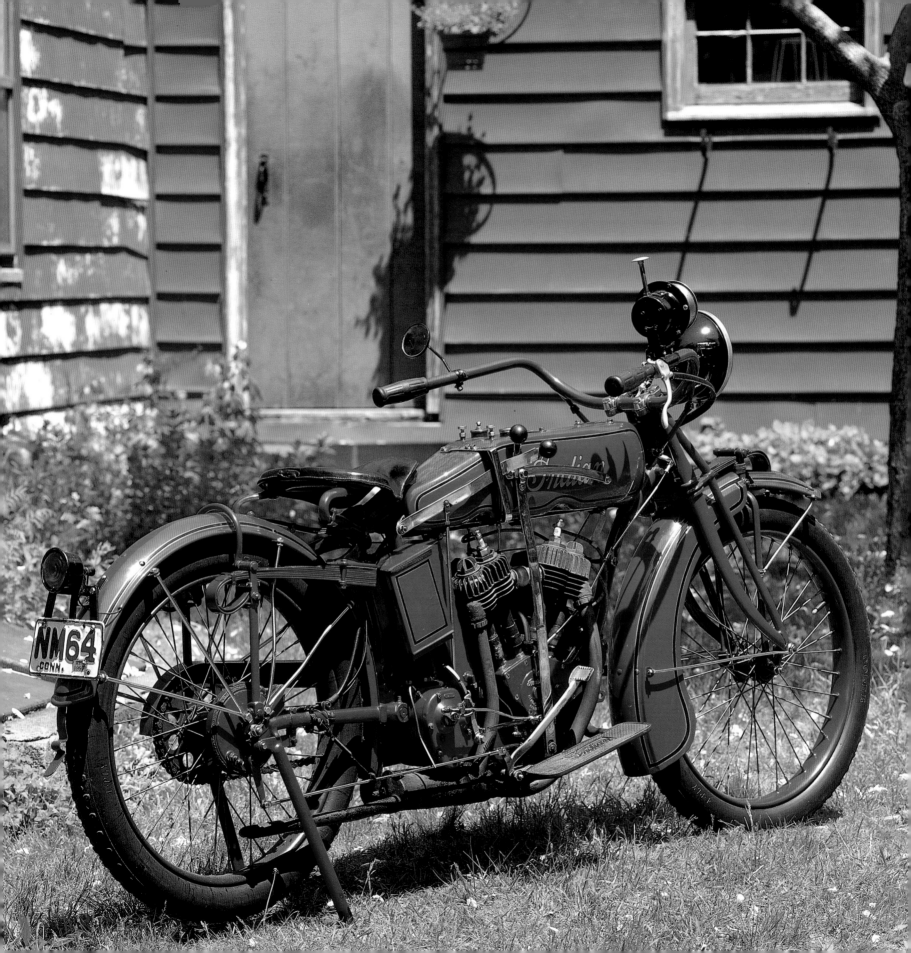

Chapter Five

The Powerplus and the Model J

New Versus Improved

Somewhere in folklore's closet there's something about how in one of the Chinese languages, the symbols for problem and opportunity are the same. There must be something like that in motorcycling, because when Hendee and Hedstrom had retired and the new owners and managers wanted something newer and less expensive and much less radical than the electric start that stopped, new head designer Gustafson was ready.

His earlier training had been with Reading-Standard, where the engineering must have been better than the ill-fated firm's record. Gustafson had brought with him some experience in design and he used it on a new and different engine, introduced late in 1915.

It was still the V-twin with the 42 degrees included angle, but he replaced the pocket valves with detachable cylinder heads and put the valves next to the pistons instead of off to one side. The sidevalve (or flathead, in the slang used then and later) was quieter and required less maintenance and was—no accident, surely—cheaper to make.

Displacement was 61ci, the traditional size for a big twin, and actual power was 16 or so horsepower, several horses more than the Hedstrom pocket-valve 61.

Indian gave the new machine the inspired name Powerplus, justified because it did have more power. It used the quarter-elliptic front spring and had the optional rear suspension, which wasn't popular. By the 1914 model year, Indian had sorted out if not quite perfected the electrics, so there were options for battery and lights (some owners still preferred the proven yet dimmer gas lights). The nicely done Powerplus had floorboards, a real clutch, and a gearbox.

There were variations in both directions, in that there was a sidevalve single, pretty much half the twin, and for racing, in which Indian was deeply involved in 1916, there was a twin and a single, both based, literally, on the new engine cases. These racing conversions came to be known as small-base eight-valves, to distinguish them from the earlier derived racing engines, the big-base series.

Harley-Davidson lived up to what was becoming its heritage by meeting the Indian challenge with an improved, rather than a new, design. William Harley wasn't exactly against innovation, as we'll see in subsequent chapters, but he didn't indulge in radical notions for no reason. Nor, by the evidence, did Ottaway, his assistant in the engineering department as well as team manager. Thus, while

Indian's Powerplus, shown here in 1917 trim, was a useful leap forward in power and in production efficiency. But rear suspension was an option. Jeff Hackett

in 1914 Indian presented the electric start that didn't work, H-D offered the step-start, which did.

Harley went against the trend in that sales were going up while motorcycle sales in general declined, to the extent that H-D could claim to be the largest exclusively motorcycle company. Indian still had the sales lead, but it also made bicycles, which is better than going out of business, the fate of scores of lesser makes.

As an interesting odd note, Harley used an engine dynamometer for tests and advertised that it was the only firm to guarantee an engine's output. In the case of the 61 cubic-inch Model J—Harley wasn't using names yet—the company promised 11 horsepower. Once H-D saw that the Indian made more power, it said the tests had shown the Model J actually made 16-plus horsepower, right on what Indian had.

A Military Miscalculation

Early history shows that Hendee and Arthur Davidson both worked hard to build their respective dealer networks and appreciated those

The 1917 Powerplus had fully valanced, as in wrap-around, front fender and an electric headlight that at least looks capable of piercing the darkest night. *Jeff Hackett*

*I*ndian's Powerplus was a logical improvement, with the more powerful sidevalve engine in the ahead-of-its-time fully suspended frame. This example is a 1915, the model's first year. *Roy Kidney/Gordy Clark*

whom they'd brought into their folds. But by 1916, Hendee was living the life of a country squire. Indian was owned by financial types, who didn't seem to have realized that the dealers were the factory's primary and most committed customers. And America was approaching World War I.

Motorcycling's military experience began before that, when Gen. "Black Jack" Pershing was chasing Mexican leader Pancho Villa back and forth across the border. Pershing happened to have with him a fleet of Harleys, and Villa was photographed on an Indian. The two disputants didn't actually chase each other on motorcycles, but the excursions did show that motorcycles were useful in the field. So when the American military began preparing to enter the war, it ordered lots and lots of motorcycles. This was in a lower key than we'd see later, in that the motorcycle makers were invited to take part; they didn't have to. Nor was there rationing of parts or limits on sales.

*T*his is Cannonball Baker, with the host of new friends that always collects when somebody sets a record, which Baker has just done. The machine is an Indian Powerplus, with the new sidevalve engine in the Cradle Spring frame. The rear suspension was an option, and not many people bought it, but surely Baker appreciated the feature. Just as surely, he appreciated his bike's twin headlights, giant horn, and sturdy odometer driven off the front hub. *Hap Alzina Archives*

*T*he Powerplus looks so new, such an advance, that it's surprising to see the hand levers all working off the side of the fuel tank, because the twist grip is yet to come. *Roy Kidney/Gordy Clark*

Harley-Davidson's big twin was in a constant state of refinement from the first. This is the 1924 version of the intake-over-exhaust engine. The single camshaft is centered in the vee, behind the driven gears. The valves are operated through a series of pivoted rocker and pushrods, with the train of gears driving the oil pump, generator, and ignition. © *Harley-Davidson Motor Company*

Electricity was becoming understood, so this Harley had full electric lights. Lower tanks had sales appeal, even if the tank needed cutouts for the intake valve rockers. *Roy Kidney/Vintage Museum*

Harley's transitions for the period included adding a clutch while keeping (until 1916) the pedals and having hand and foot clutch control. This example, which was discovered in such good condition it hasn't been restored, has the optional three-speed gearbox. *Roy Kidney/Vintage Museum*

Indian's management decided to go all out. They thought they could maximize profits by selling all possible production to the military, with none of this foolish sales and advertising effort.

Harley-Davidson went the other way and agreed to provide any motorcycles the military might want to order but at the same time kept civilian production going. Harley-Davidson dealers would have something to do during the war. Indian's dealers were left to fend for themselves.

Only a probationary poetic license is required to say that Indian won the war: it got most of the military business and presumably got the profit the plan had predicted. According to Jerry Hatfield's research, the U.S.government took 70,000 motorcycles. Of those, 20,000 came from Harley-Davidson and most of the rest came from Indian.

The actual models were primarily Powerplus and J-series twins. The manufacturers made few changes for the armed services, as the motorcycles weren't intended or used for actual combat and the conditions in Europe—mud or dust or both at once—were pretty much the same as those in rural America in 1918.

There was one small and unhappy omen. The defense department initiated a program to develop a military motorcycle, to be produced by all the rival makes and to use the various features the procuring agencies thought best. It was called the Liberty Motor and it combined this from Indian, that from H-D, and something else from Excelsior. When the plan was ready and the war was over, the whole thing was canceled. And when the shootings stopped and peace and prosperity came back, Indian and Harley-Davidson were neck-and-neck.

*T*his is real road racing, eh? The group, consisting of a pair of Indian twins, three Excelsior Ace fours, and at least one Harley-Davidson, is obviously ready for some speed. Just as obviously this is a public road, they aren't formally organized, and the police are keeping order, not writing tickets. Best of all, these are the only guys you'll ever see with a good reason for wearing their caps back to front. *Cycle World*

RIGHT
*S*idecars remained a viable option until the price of four wheels plus top and electric starting came within reach of the working man. After that, rigs were either for sport or the man who simply couldn't bear driving a car. *Cycle World*

*T*he operator is having fun tipping the chair into the air, while the occupant puts up with it and the horses don't seem to be panicked. The motorcycle is a Powerplus and because that's the kind of guy he was, Hap Alzina has to be the prankster behind this stunt. *Hap Alzina Archives*

*P*owerplus engine was as tidy as science could make it, but routing the controls, as in the levers and rods from the grips down to the carburetor and ignition, took lots of parts. The oil tank, with convenient plunger handle for pumping, is aft of the rear barrel, in front of the battery. The start lever has been moved from the crankcase rearward, outboard of the clutch.

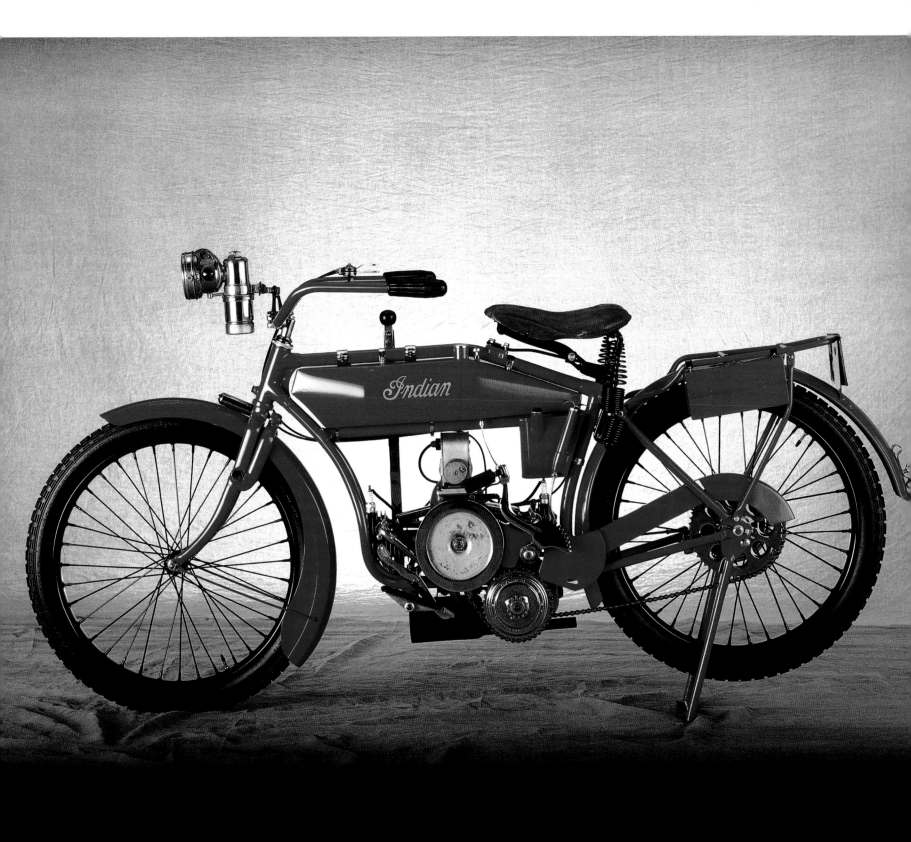

Chapter Six

The Model O and The Model WJ Sport Twin

The Little Engines That Couldn't

Along about the time motorcycling went into a nearly fatal slump, close to the end of the Harley-Indian rivalry, critics who didn't know much history took it upon themselves to carp about how things would have been different if the Big Two had been more experimental and daring and hadn't just cranked out the same old stuff year after year. Not true. Not by a whole lot.

Because the motorcycle began as a motorized bicycle and was so obviously a practical way to get about cheap, the makers were slow to realize that people would rather have things comfy than cheap. Thus, when the car got the electric start and permanent top and the price went down every year, cars sold like hotdogs at halftime and motorcycles fell by the wayside.

Indian's counterpunch was the Featherweight, a two-stroke single offered in 1916. OK, it was mostly a bicycle, with a solid mounted rear wheel and the old-style pivoting spring-clip forks. But it had a three-speed gearbox and no pedals.

What the Featherweight, coded Model K, lacked, was sales appeal. It sat on a few showroom floors for a year and was taken out of the catalog. The replacement was a clever notion, an opposed twin whose cylinders were aligned with the wheel-base, one in front and the other trailing. Some of the cycle parts were shared or derived from the K, but the frame was different and the wheelbase was longer. Displacement was 15.7 cubic inches, which simply wasn't enough. Adding to that, the model was somehow named the Model O, which unkind critics inside Indian and out instantly converted to the Model Nothing. But the true handicap must have been that it was, well, too practical, small, and quiet. The Model Nothing was on the market for the 1917, 1918, and 1919 seasons and it, too, was withdrawn after dismal sales.

Strangely, the horizontal fore and aft four-stroke twin had appeared earlier, with the English Douglas, where it performed and sold well; apparently the English market was different. But the Douglas had clearly attracted American attention because in 1919, work having been interrupted by the war, Harley-Davidson introduced a new machine that was as much like the Model O and the Douglas as it was unlike anything H-D had made before or has made since.

The new Harley followed the Indian concept, as in fore-and-aft twin, but the W Series Sport Twin, to use the full designation, was usefully larger—36 cubic inches or 600cc—and thus had more power

Indian's opposed fore-and-aft twin is so small it barely looks like an engine. The cartridge front suspension and the gas-powered headlight were out of date by 1916, and one suspects Indian was using up leftover parts. Roy Kidney/Vintage Museum

The Model O engine was compact, with the crankcases kept small by hanging the flywheel outboard. The small shields on each side of the flywheel protect the pushrods for the valves, which are horizontal in the cylinders. The basic kick start, requiring the operator to follow through or else, will stay with Indian up to the very end. *Cycle World*

than the Model O. The W was rated at 6 horsepower and probably had more power than that.

The W Series had a keystone frame, with the long, thin engine's crankcase serving to bridge and stiffen the frame tubes. Rear suspension was solid, while the forks were rocking-trailing links, not William Harley's design and not much like anything seen on a rival of the time. There was a three-speed gearbox with a shift and foot clutch. Engine and gearbox were one unit, again not H-D practice, with the gears above the engine. The drivetrain was enclosed, and there was even a front brake, which was a radical move for the time, even on cars.

Harley's marketing and timing were better than Indian's. The latter's lightweight campaign was interrupted by war, while the W Series arrived with

Harley's middleweight was unique and not just for its engine. The chain was enclosed, so it ran cool and clean; the gearbox was above the crankcase, so the engine was low; and the crossover forks aren't like anything from the time. (H-D hillclimbers had a similar system ten years later.) *Roy Kidney/Vintage Museum*

peacetime and was presented just as people were looking for ways to spend money.

Not only that, the W was promoted. A Sport Twin was the first motorcycle to scale California's Mount Baldy. Other examples set cross-country records: Canada to Mexico for one, Chicago to Denver for another.

Early in its production run, the Sport Twin was the best-selling solo motorcycle on the American market. And when Europe got back on its feet, the Sport Twin was Harley's best-selling export model. But in 1923, with lofts and lots packed with unsold W Series Sport Twins, the model was taken off the market.

Now we come to human vagaries. Early in the 1920s, motorcycling's moguls wondered why the public wasn't buying motorcycles the way they had before the war. They commissioned a survey, but according to historian Harry Sucher, the various moguls were not fond of each other and the very fact of the survey had to be kept quiet lest any of the big guys be caught knowing the other guy's business.

So it happened that the results of the survey were a long time coming. When they did arrive, the results showed that the public wasn't buying motorcycles, said the moguls with straight faces, because they were too loud, noisy, fast, and not practical. What the public wanted, the public supposedly said, was motorcycles like the Model O and the WJ. What management at Indian and Harley-Davidson said about that we don't officially know and probably wouldn't print if we did.

This was or was not, take your pick, coincidence, but at about the time of World War I, both Indian and Harley-Davidson introduced models that were radically different from what they'd been building and surprisingly like each other. Indian's Model O was smaller and lighter and more like a bicycle, while Harley-Davidson's Sport Twin was a full-sized motorcycle. Roy Kidney/Vintage Museum

Chapter Seven

The Scout and the Model D

Indian Takes the Lead

Speaking of blatant revisionist history, let's say that Daimler's rig was done to test an engine, rather than invent the motorcycle. Hedstrom, in contrast, did his prototype to see if motor and bicycle would be combined for practical advantage, which is to say the motorcycle was invented in 1901, rather than 1885.

Assuming that, if we celebrate the Motorcycle's First Century in 2001, and if we make a list of the important models built during that century, there is no list so short that it wouldn't have to have the Indian Scout.

Not only that, but the Scout wasn't just a critical and commercial success, it was better than anything Harley-Davidson could offer *and* it was better than Indian's management had expected.

How so? Reflect on the dismal history of the ill-fated Hendee Special, still a blot on Indian's ledger when the Great War ended and the abandoned dealers got even by deserting. Hendee and Hedstrom had retired, the moneymen were in charge. The two-stroke single and fore-and-aft twin weren't selling, and the Powerplus, otherwise an excellent machine, was still lumbered with rear suspension that cost more than it brought in.

Salvation came from the mind and hands of Charles Franklin, a man who seems to have been destined to design great motorcycles. Franklin was born in Ireland, and was a racer. He signed onto the Indian team for the glorious times at the Isle of Man and on the English tracks. He was a degreed engineer, in a day when most designers, Hedstrom for

OPPOSITE
*H*arley's factory team, in action on the banked boards. That the factory lined up these guys in formation and had the photographer record the parade indicates they planned to use the wins and the engineering to their advantage. The huge tracks (mile-plus in some instances) were surely as intimidating from the saddle as they are here. © *Harley-Davidson Motor Company*

*T*he original Scout was compact and muscular and appealed to the enthusiast. Kick start had been moved from the front left to the right rear. *Jeff Hackett*

he began with the by-then-classic Indian configuration of a V-twin with 42-degrees included angle. He continued the sidevalve top end of the Powerplus, which worked perfectly well on the fuel and the engine speeds of the day.

He made two major improvements. First, while the older Indian big twin used one central camshaft working the four valves from an angle, the Scout engine had two camshafts, one below each cylinder. Carefully sited rocker arms let one lobe serve both the intake and exhaust valves, in sequence. There were fewer parts to flex and better breathing because the valve sequences were better controlled.

The older Indians and the Harley V-twins had the engine bolted to the frame, and the gearbox bolted to the frame, bridged by a case that held a chain primary drive. Adjusting the primary chain meant sliding the gearbox in its mounts, which is another way to say that there was more stuff to go wrong and more need to spend time maintaining.

Franklin did the drivetrain as a rigid assembly, with engine, gearbox, and primary case as one, with the drive from flywheels to input shaft done with three helical gears: three so the engine would revolve in the same direction as the motorcycle's wheels. This was durable, quiet, and expensive but worth it.

The engine displaced 37 cubic inches, or 600cc, which just happened to match that of Harley's sport twin, the fore-and-aft model that came after Indian's version. The Sport Twin was introduced in 1918 and the Scout in 1919 as a 1920 model. Harley's middleweight was gone by 1923; the Scout, albeit much changed, would meet and compete until the end, and even then there were customers still in line.

The Scout's engine and gearbox went into a

Indian's original Scout had the engineering to go with its wonderful name. The Scout used a peppy, midsize engine that improved on the larger Powerplus in a lighter, lower, and more agile frame and running gear. Jeff Hackett

one, had taught themselves through books and experience. He came to the United States and on the strength of his engineering and racing credentials, was hired by Indian.

Franklin knew his engines. He also knew there'd be concern for cost, so

The Harley singles came ready for road or track. This is the overhead cam version, with the low bars and sketchy fenders worn for racing at the time. The road model looks, well, sort of dull and didn't sell, while the racing single was a longtime winner. © Harley-Davidson Motor Company

new frame, with the familiar leaf spring front suspension and the rear wheel rigidly mounted. Rear suspension was still standard on the Powerplus, but the model had few takers.

The Scout became an overnight success. One is tempted to ask why. Didn't we just learn that smaller engines didn't appeal to the public? Wasn't the Harley opposed twin, same displacement as the Scout, failing just as the Scout appeared? Yes and yes.

One factor has to have been the name: Scout. It's right out of western folklore and the Boy's Book of Derring-Do. It's a great name and ranks with Sportster, Black Shadow, and Thunderbird.

Next, folklorists have always wondered if there's something in the cadence of the V-twin, the galloping beat of the cowboy (or Indian) racing across the plains.

A bit fanciful? We're probably closer to the Scout's secret if we note that history makes it perfectly clear that those who like motorcycles like to look at engines. And it helps if those engines are impressive.

Check the Sport Twin and the Model Nothing. Notice there's lots of empty space within the parameters of the frames. The engines are sunk to the bottom of the frames, and they don't much look like engines. Check out the Scout. The frame is full of a By-Daimler Engine. OK, it sounds funny at first, but there has to be something to it.

In any event, the Scout was an instant success, with orders coming in faster than the factory could fill them and attracting back some of the dealers who'd gone away during the war.

And what of the rivals? (There's a reason for the plural.) Harley-Davidson was developing a habit that would eventually be a virtue, but at this point looked foolish. It didn't directly challenge the Scout. This looks odd. H-D was in the catbird seat, with a better dealer network, stronger sales, and a more rationally occupied factory. They got out of the bicycle business just about the time the non-founding, nonriding managers at Indian got into the car parts business, so Harley gained efficiency as fast as Indian lost it.

The Singles Scene

Both companies persisted in the notion that there was a market for practical, as in cheap and sturdy, motorcycles. In 1925 both brands introduced new singles, both displacing 21 cubic inches or 350cc. In keeping with tradition, the Indian had a name, the Prince, and the Harley didn't. But they were alike, in size and power and in coming as either a sidevalve or an overhead valve configuration.

At this time, both H-D and Indian were looking overseas. They were selling strongly across both ponds, with the big twins becoming the machine of choice for sportsmen in England and Australia and the singles doing well in the commercial markets. The Prince was even built with a hand clutch and a footshift for the export market, proving it wasn't that Americans didn't know about such things, it was that (as we'll see much later) the American buyer didn't want them.

And of course H-D matched Indian in the big twin market. But during this time, the early and middle 1920s, Harley didn't offer a middleweight

Albert "Shrimp" Burns, aboard a small-base eight-valve Indian. There was no production requirement or even a rule for the board track machines, which were always ridden by professionals, and the frame of Burn's Indian didn't come from the factory, or if it did, it wasn't the customer model. Burns died in a crash at Toledo, Ohio, in 1921. The board tracks were deadly, which helped turn the sport into a spectacle. *Hap Alzina Archives*

ties, a third one can be too small to win, but still large enough to influence.

The third party then was Excelsior. The Chicago-based maker was owned by Ignaz Schwinn, who was a bicycle magnate, a thriving and successful businessman, and a true motorcycle enthusiast. Excelsiors were never big sellers, but they were good machines. One of the probably true racing myths is that it was the Excelsiors that pushed Hedstrom into building the eight-valve Indian racers.

Excelsior stunned the racing world in 1920 with an overhead cam 61-cubic-inch V-twin, even though a racing crash killed the make's star, Bob Perry, and caused Schwinn to lose some of his enthusiasm for racing. But the real history was made in 1925, with the introduction of the Super X, an intake-over-exhaust V-twin displacing 45 cubic inches, or 750cc. This came before club racing as we know it now, and it came at a time when most racing was done with the pro bikes, the 21- or 30–50-cubic-inch singles, or the big 61- or 74-cubic-inch twins. The Super X was faster than its rivals.

A bunch of the guys seem to have ridden into the country and borrowed a hill to climb. They've taken off their headlights and untied their ties, and the man with the firmest jaw is going to win. *Cycle World*

twin. Instead, as the records from the board meetings revealed much later, it kept an eye on the market.

A New Class

The sporting middleweight market promptly got better, which introduced a spoiler. In business as in politics, when you have two big par-

*T*here was also professional hillclimbing, with machines as specialized as the example shown here, the overhead valve version of the road-going Indian, in a custom frame that moved everything back a useful few inches. *Jeff Hackett*

Back in the Wigwam at Springfield, there were plans. The official Indian myth says that lots of police departments liked the 37-cubic-inch Scout because it was much easier to start than the big twins. But cars were getting faster and the little Scout couldn't keep up, the story goes, and the police departments asked for more power.

Franklin knew about overhead cams and valves, but he also knew there were money problems, so the problem was solved by making a Scout 45. The new and larger engine was announced for 1927, which was timed perfectly to counter the Super X. Still a sidevalve engine, the enlarged Scout had more power and would in fact run with the Excelsior.

Harley Strikes Back

As hindsight would have predicted, the singles were popular enough to stay in the catalog for a couple of years, but that was all they did.

Harley-Davidson had been taking notes. Their intake-over-exhaust engines were good examples of an old, perhaps even outmoded, design being kept viable through attention to detail. They had made enlargements and improvements over the years—see chapter nine for more detail—but it was clear by the mid-1920s that they needed new designs. It was probably just as clear that overhead valves would give more power but would require more maintenance and more money for extra parts.

Thus, while William Harley authorized and built some interesting prototypes and did a bunch of studies, the founders decided the way to go was a new set of sidevalve V-twins, middleweights, and heavyweights.

Historian Jerry Hatfield, who had access to the H-D files for the period, reports that the middleweight project began in 1926. That sounds right, as it comes soon after the singles project and would have been a predictable response to the success of the Scout. Not only that, the size and shape of the cycle components for the new middleweight hints that when the work began, the new Harley engine dis-

placed 37 cubic inches, the same size as the retired Sport Twin and the original Scout.

But when it came on the market in 1928, it was a 45, just like the Excelsior and the newer Scout, and fit right into Harley's line-up, between the singles and the big twins.

In general, Harley and Indian were closely matched. The Scout had a larger bore and shorter stroke, which in theory meant it could be revved higher and safer, while the Harley 45's smaller bore and longer stroke allowed less space above the piston, meaning a higher practical compression ratio.

One subtle difference, not for the first time, was that while the Indian was named Scout, next to Prince, Chief, and Standard, the Harley was designated the Model D, in plain version, DL with higher compression ratio, and DS for the D engine in a frame with lugs for sidecar mounting.

More important, where the Scout had a camshaft for each cylinder, with rockers and levers between the lobes and the valve stems, the D engine used an arc of four one-lobe shafts, each sited directly below the valve it controlled. This required an elaborate geartrain, which is why the space for the camshafts and gears is called the gearcase in H-D's lexicon. The same train of gears was used for the oil pump and the timed breather for the crankcase, the generator, and the ignition timer. This was an expensive way to run things, and

The overhead valve 750 was coded DAH. Basically it was a conversion of the sidevalve 750. There were two valves per cylinder, but the exhaust valves fed two ports each, which is the reason for all the exhaust pipes.

Indian Laughs First

*U*nlikely though it seems, the personal and comical aspects of our feud began with a caricature. The commercial rivalry of course originated as soon as Harley-Davidson became a major manufacturer, and the sporting contest began when both makes entered early competitions. But mockery was an added factor.

Consider first, that when the Greek playwrights invented the stage play back in the dawn of literacy and the arts, their stage directions included the use of—how does one say this politely?—the Single Digit. The Flying Finger. Honest. To paraphrase, when the script called for one character to disrespect another, the Greeks had a gesture for it.

This has to have been because even back then and perhaps earlier still, people didn't like to be disrespected, which inspired other people to figure out just how to do it with maximum effect. Thus, the finger. Or mooning the crowd, which also goes way back. First, the attacker makes a joke and then asks innocently, Can't you take a joke?, because of course most of us can't.

So? So when George Hendee named his motorcycle, he did it with respect. Nothing was more American, he felt, than the First American. The artwork used by the company for badges and logo and such was respectful, even dignified.

Laughing Indian logo courtesy of Jerry Greer's Indian Engineering

The time was one of strong political feelings, which led to forceful political campaigning and cartooning and from somewhere, back about 1910, factory literature appeared with artwork of a different nature. This was another Indian, who was laughing, make that sneering, at whomever was the target.

He was making a joke or mocking somebody or something, and he came to be known as the Laughing Indian. The emblem appeared on paper and then on patches. Presumably the patches were to be put on jackets. But some of the racers put the patches on the seats of their racing britches. Right. They mooned the opposition, minus the chill factor of course.

Racing was evolving into something nobody had expected. At first, speed and durability were proof of progress, as when Hedstrom stormed that hill back in Springfield, or when Walter Davidson turned in the perfect score in the reliability run, or when Cannonball Baker and Indian set records coast to coast.

Then racing became a spectacle. The banked board tracks were fast beyond expectations: In 1922, Jim Davis turned a lap of 110.67 mile per hour on Beverly Hills mile track. That's still the fastest one-mile lap ever recorded. But there were fatalities, which the newspapers made the most of. Motorcycle racing

it was noisier than a simpler system would have been. But it worked. It worked so well that the same system is still being used in Harley-Davidson's 1997 middleweight Sportsters.

The most obvious (at the time) change in the cycle parts was that the Model D, and the rival Scout, had front brakes. It sounds odd to say this now, but front brakes, for cars as well as motorcycles, were a long time coming. High speeds back then were legal on the open road, and the open roads weren't often paved, so in some ways the front brake was as tricky as the folklore of the time portrayed it. The myth of the day was that front brakes were a bad thing, to be

used with extreme caution if at all. This blatantly false belief lived for 50 or 60 years in riders who carefully never used the front brake; "Throw ya right over the bars," they told impressionable youngsters.

The Model D had the conventional Harley leading-link front suspension, beefed up to handle the added loads from the brake. The rear wheel was solidly mounted, a habit H-D wouldn't overcome for several more generations. Because the new engine was packed into a frame done first for the big Harley single, the generator was upright, to the front left of the front cylinder, which led to quips about the three-cylinder Harley from the

became famous for speed, skill, and death. It was as if all the public knew of horse was rodeo: while the riders might be heroic, it wouldn't cause people to want to have a horse, or ride one to work.

During the same time period, makes disappeared as fast as they arrived on the market. By the 1920s, there were three brands in racing: Harley, Indian, and Excelsior, and the last didn't have a full team. Racing became specialized as the sanctioning body limited national events to the smaller engines, full-race singles that ordinary people didn't ride. The lesser classes were production-based, hill climbs and TT mostly and were open to the larger twins. (There were no formal rules, but because 25 examples were considered a fair claim to production, when Excelsior replaced its intake-over-exhaust 750 V-twin with an overhead valve 750 V-twin, Harley and Indian both built 26 overhead valve 750s, which were not sold to the public and were used for at least the next ten years for racing and experimentation.)

There were serious imbalances. H-D won all the nationals in 1921 and then disbanded the factory team. Indian ruled in the next two seasons and went on to double the revenge, taking all the nationals in 1928 and 1929.

What mattered here most was that motorcycle racing attracted the daredevils and was ignored by everybody else. It can be argued that the racing speeds hurt the sport because all anybody heard about were injuries and deaths. Next, a sort of under-

class had been established, which included events for daring riders of less than professional status and/or skill, on the bikes they rode every day.

For the conclusion here, having just two brands in competition fostered the us versus them mentality. When six makes were on the line, you could root for your guys, but when there were just two, you also had someone to root against. And then Indian's marketing department put the Laughing Indian into general circulation. Indian announced a club, the Laughing Indian Club. It was for owners of Indians, not surprisingly, and the members got Laughing Indian badges and patches to put on their machines and themselves.

The top members of this club were owners who'd helped their dealer sell at least five Indians to other riders. Those who did this got a special badge, identifying the badge holder as an Ace. The name came from World War I, but many years later, when restorers began rooting through the proverbial barns and found these badges, they had a heck of a time figuring out why an Indian fender had an Ace badge on it.

What had been created by all this, not on purpose but with lasting effect, was what the poet C. S. Lewis referred to as the Inner Circle, a boundary inside which the members of a group were, and the others, the outsiders, weren't.

From now on, mostly in fun and good sportsmanship but sometimes not, it would be Indian versus Harley-Davidson.

other camps. More important in actual use, the D had twin headlights, and the generator wasn't powerful enough to keep the battery up if the lights were used all the time.

Actual production of the D series started in mid-1928, with the line moving slowly because everything wasn't sorted out yet, and the first production examples were listed as 1929 models. It was good, solid work, and if the Model D wasn't ahead of its time, it was there just in time.

*S*uper X was Excelsior's sport model, and it kept both the larger firms nervous, perhaps even envious. The 45-cubic-inch Super X was more than a match for the rival 61s, while the X's unit construction pioneered the idea in the United States. *Roy Kidney/Vintage Museum*

Chapter Eight

The Chief and the JDH

Great Leaps and Gradual Increments

Excepting only the experiences of Sam Langford and maybe Sugar Ray Robinson on his best days, few rules in sport are more easily proven than the boxing axiom: A good big man will always whip a good little man. So it is with motorcycles, magnified by some accidents of history.

At some ill-defined point on the time chart, motorcycle marketing became a matter of niche, as in sports or touring, big or little. But that wasn't the idea when the industry/sport began. Instead, there were singles, then twins, triples (only a handful, admittedly, and from guys like Glenn Curtiss, who was first so often he was as frequently by himself, way out in left field), and fours.

Indian and Harley-Davidson evolved their V-twins, and engine size increased in ratio with the need for power and the ability of the engines to hold up under the stress of making that power.

The first of our happy accidents was that in Europe, where motor vehicles were the playthings of the rich and taxation was a way to express class envy, engines were taxed on their size, which made it more practical to select a displacement, the smaller the better, and tune the small engine to the required power output.

America was more democratic, the machines more practical, distances more distant, and taxes levied in different ways. Motorcycle motors developed in what's known as the aircraft method, where the designer begins with what power is needed and sizes the engine to develop that power with minimum stress.

Or, as the hot rod crowd put it much later, "You can't beat cubic inches."

The little V-twins from our heroes and the others grew right along with the number of paved miles and the need for a second seat, a sidecar, lights, or luggage.

Hail to the Chief

The ill-fated Hendee Special provided some evidence as to where to go next, and the spectacularly successful Scout provided the rest, while the Powerplus, as noted, had a new, sidevalve engine in the older style, with optional rear suspension and frame. This was a stopgap.

For model year 1922 Indian introduced the Chief. It was a wonderful name, surely the best name an Indian could have. It was also a clearly evolutionary motorcycle. The engine was a sidevalve, which had been proven already by the Powerplus and Scout. The Powerplus, by the way, with the old frame and rear suspension, remained in the catalog for a few more years, but it was renamed as the Standard, surely

While Indian was making the same thing in different sizes, Harley-Davidson made variations of the same thing in different sizes. Shown here is a 1928 JD, J for intake-over-exhaust twin with one camshaft for the four valves, D for 74ci. There's a front brake, but the lever is on the left because the throttle is on the right and they hadn't yet needed to have one hand do several controls at the same time. Roy Kidney/Vintage Museum

The JD's stylishly low saddle tanks required the notches for valve gear. The speedometer on the tank join is driven by a gear on the rear hub, and it has one of the earliest fishtail exhausts, patterned after a racing device that supposedly kept noise down without restricting flow. Paint is—yawn—Brewster green, a variation on the earlier olive. Roy Kidney/Vintage Museum

Sidecars hadn't quite lost the battle by 1926. This Chief, which was designed with haulage in mind from the outset, has been fitted with not only a chair but with weather equipment, as in top and windshield. There's a useful spotlight and a running light, so oncoming traffic will know this motorcycle is wider than normal. And the passenger gets a step and a door. Even so, the fully enclosed heater-equipped sedan will soon become the family vehicle of choice. Hap Alzina Archives

because there was concern that the Powerplus label hinted it had more power than Chief. Which it didn't.

Charles Franklin, the man behind the Scout, was now chief engineer, and he drew up, in essence, a larger and more powerful Scout. The engine still displaced 61 cubic inches, same as the Standard, with the expected 42 degree included angle, but the Chief produced more power. It was semi-unit, with gear primary and the new engine in a new frame, with a lower seat and more graceful tanks and fenders. By now it should go without saying that the Chief had a three-speed gearbox, handshift, and foot clutch and came with lights and generator, albeit the ignition was magneto. A stock Chief in good health would hit 90 miles per hour, which in 1922 had to have been more than enough. At least.

HEP Big Chief

That subtitle may be politically suspect, as in slurs on various groups and the Heap Big Injun dialog in the early western movies. In historical fact, it was an accident. The motorcycle makers were still figuring out how to describe their products. In the 1920s, Harleys used letters F and J for their twins, to be introduced shortly, while Indian won the day with names like Chief, Scout, and Prince.

Even so, there was a code. Thus in 1923, when the original Chief was joined by a 74-cubic-inch version (and the Standard quietly disappeared, taking rear suspension with it), Indian coded the 61 as the HE Chief and the 74 as the HEP Big Chief. That's a quote, and surely they didn't mean it to come out as corny dialog.

Bore and stroke for the 61 was 3 1/8x3 31/32 inches, and the 74 measured 3 1/4x4 7/16 inches. Listed weight for the Chief in either displacement was 425 pounds, a hefty increase over the Scout, and wheelbase was 60.5 inches.

The Chief was as instant a sales success as the Scout had been. Historian Jerry Hatfield has charts for all this and says that although the Scout got all the ads and the raves, in fact the 61 Chief and then the 74 version led the sales race, for Indian at any rate, but we'll deal with that in due course.

Speaking of course, we are on course, as the free market and good design had by the mid-1920s established that the big, under-stressed twin was the motorcycle of choice for the daring few who chose to ride. America was a strong exporter then, which in turn led to barriers being built elsewhere, notably England and Japan, which in its turn led to the Depression but that, too, comes later.

The Start of the Finish

Here begins the sad part. By the mid-1920s, the motorcycle business had gone, well, flat. Harley-Davidson had the largest plant and workforce, then

Indian, then—and far behind—Excelsior. What the three surviving American motorcycle makers also had in common was too much plant for the demand for their product.

The good news for Indian was that the engineering staff, still headed by Franklin, was strong and talented. More useful, the engineers were allowed to improve the bikes, witness the larger Chief, the addition of a front brake, the evolution (can we say that about Indian?) of the thriving Scout.

Further, Indian had a good little single, the Prince, which doesn't figure much in the feud but which did sell overseas and for commercial purpose,

perhaps the original paper boy bike, to use the snide remark made later to riders of small Harleys. Indian could and did advertise a full product line, from single to small twin to big twin to four.

The bad news was that Indian's founders had retired and the men who'd bought them out were businessmen. The best of the managers in that day was a man named Frank Weschler, a nonbiker but an experienced and ethical executive.

The owners of Indian didn't really know they owned a motorcycle company. They thought they owned a factory and controlled a corporation. Thus, when Indian made money, Weschler voted to put the

Then Harley-Davidson introduced optional paint, for instance red, white, and blue. This is another JD, but with a dazzling paint scheme. This is authentic and verified. The buyer could have such paint for the asking, but he had to ask. The options weren't in the catalog or the ads or even mentioned in H-D's magazine. *James Wear/Ross van Etten*

money back into the product and the bank. The owners said no. Instead, they diversified into car parts, refrigerators, and industry gear and even, a bit later, a minicar with a Chief powerplant.

As if that wasn't bad enough, the directors voted to get into the stock market, using Indian as security. That was get-away-with-it legal then and yes, you were right when you stopped in your tracks and shouted, "Look out! The market will crash in 1929!" In 1928 and 1929, mostly because the non-motorcycle products were not good and didn't sell, Indian lost better than a million dollars.

If this part of Indian history was a graph, there'd be two lines. The one labeled product would start in the middle and go up, the one labeled management would start at the top and slump to the bottom.

Meanwhile, in Milwaukee

The Harley-Davidson chart would begin with product in the middle and management on the high side, too. Thing is, the H-D lines don't cross. Harley's good move was the decision to support the dealers and the riders during the war, which as noted gave The Motor Company an edge when buyers and peace and prosperity returned.

The bad move, well, wait. It's not fair to say the Sport Twin was a bad move. It was a good machine, it simply didn't sell. What the cautious founders did, therefore, was build what they knew would se11, which was Big Twins.

This was evolution long before H-D used the word for promotion. The emphasis and development was on the intake-over-exhaust twins, which grew from 50 to 61 to 74 cubic inches during the course of their run, which lasted until 1930.

Historian Hatfield documents this development and establishes that the actual basic design was set by 1915 or close to that and simply got better with age and technology from there. This isn't to say the improvements weren't worth it. There was even some spin-off from racing, which happens a lot less often than the racing department wants the accounting office to believe.

The 1929 Js got dual headlights and a voltage regulator of sorts, a control so the rider could up the output if the lights began to draw down the battery. The four-pipe dual exhaust system was also used for one year. It seems to have worked too well and made the engine too quiet. *James Wear/Ross van Etten*

This is the top of the 1929 line, with dual headlights and four-pipe exhaust but the paint is black to olive green and the larger and flatter timing case cover identifies it as a JDH, which translates as a J series engine, D for 74 cubic inchesand H for the two camshafts, one beneath each set of valves. *Roy Kidney/Vintage Museum*

The early eight-valve racing engines were built atop the best of the intake-over-exhaust lower ends, which were coded with numbers that began in the 500s. The eight-valve engines used one camshaft with four lobes, while the originals had two lobes and rockers to allow for the shared parts. But beginning in 1917, all the J engines, road or racing, got the four-lobe camshafts.

Even better, in 1928, the one shaft with four lobes became two shafts, one below each cylinder, with two lobes each. On that occasion H was added to the J, for 61, or JD for the 74. The improved version went into the enthusiast's vocabulary as the two-cam, nevermind that English teachers and engineers know the cam is the bumpy part, so both engines are four cam, but one is two-shaft. (That's more learning than we asked for, and two-cam will be used here.)

In an early display of marketing skill, H-D kept the earlier version, the one-cam J engine, in production, not as a rival to the JH, but as another choice. The first rule of salesmanship is, never give the mark a chance to say no, so the pitch at the Harley store was, Would you like the 61 or the 74? One camshaft or two? The plain J or the JL? With larger valves, smaller wheels shared with the two-cam versions, and shorter handlebars, the

JL was one of the first sport bikes. There was also a choice of pistons, with A in the title standing for aluminum alloy, or B, meaning cast-iron alloy.

As a historical note, in 1924 the gasoline guys introduced high-test, leaded, ethyl gas, which 1) cured the dreaded knock and ping; 2) allowed higher compression ratios and thus really did give more power and efficiency for minimum cost, as close to a free lunch as was ever seen; and 3) doomed the sidevalve engine because higher octane gas allowed the overhead valve engines to improve on their compression ratios but the sidevalve engine, by its nature, can't do that. But the sidevalves didn't die until years later.

More important at the time, while Indian did have a full model range and said as much, and the single, the large and small twins, and later the four did span the market, the market turned out to be sort of a bell curve.

Harley-Davidson offered a line of small singles, 21 cubic inches with sidevalve or overhead valve tops, and a choice of battery/coil or magneto ignition, but these were mostly for export, and while they earned some money, they had little influence on the market or our rivalry. And as mentioned elsewhere, Harley's management looked at the histories of the Ace, Henderson, Excelsior, and Cleveland fours, and didn't go into that cave.

H-D's main effort was with the twins, the middleweights, and the heavyweights, which was where the buyers were concentrated. It didn't hurt that the configuration was a good match for conditions of the day. According to those who were there, a perfectly stock JDH, the two-cam 74, would top out at 85 miles per hour right off the showroom floor.

Improvements were a good business. The factory had some options including racing versions of the 61 done by the team and by private tuners. One popular modification was a carefully shaped chunk of iron that could be fitted to the top of the combustion chamber. The compression ratio was raised to 6.5:1 and a JDH so modified would deliver 50 horsepower, which worked out to an honest 100 miles per hour on the road, which in

While H-D didn't make as much of paint options as it could have, the company did offer extras. This JDH has a luggage rack, while the buyer skipped the tank-mount speedometer. And Harley has presented the seat on a sliding tube, while the same-era Indian Chief still has only springs. *Roy Kidney/Vintage Museum*

By the 1920s the founding Harley and Davidsons had become the prosperous industrialists shown here. From left: William Davidson, Walter Davidson, Arthur Davidson, and William Harley. © *Harley-Davidson Motor Company*

those days was still pretty much open. And in 1928, the big twins got front brakes.

This isn't to say Harley-Davidson was taking things for granted. Notes from the meetings show the founders were well aware of the success Indian was having with the Scout, and at the annual meeting for 1927, Walter Davidson mentioned in a canny, casual way, that work was being done on a "small twin."

But, probably as important as its concentration on the models that sold and on planning the next move was Harley-Davidson's plodding, not-so-common sense. Remember how Indian's owners acted when they were in the chips? In 1921, Harley-Davidson was in the soup. There'd been a sales slump and the dealers had more bikes on hand than they could sell. They closed the plant for a month to clear out the inventory, and the founders cut their pay by 15 percent, to save money and surely to let

the furloughed workers know they weren't the only ones making sacrifices.

In 1921, H-D lost money. Some of the loss was due to the sales slump. But not all. The company had borrowed money to pay for the expanded plant, the largest motorcycle factory in the world. So when times got tough, they took a loss and paid off the loan.

Gambling the company's money is one kind of courage. Betting on your own future is another kind. And there are no prizes for guessing which of the two will pay off later.

Chapter Nine

The Indian Four

An Ace in the Sleeve

Remember the Sherlock Holmes story in which the dog didn't bark and only Holmes realized how important the watchdog's silence was?

Same idea here. This is an account of the rivalry between Harley-Davidson and Indian. All those who know a bit about motorcycle history could fairly say, Hey?! How can there be a chapter about the Indian Four when Harley-Davidson never produced a four of its own? That, Holmes would note if he hadn't retired to keep bees, may have been the important part. Sherlock or not, the story of the American four-cylinder motorcycle is more sad than it is short.

Four cylinders are naturally smoother and more elegant than one, two, or three, so there were fours on the market from pioneer days on, notably in the United States from the Pierce family that also made the elegant Pierce-Arrow motorcar.

Then came the Henderson brothers, who made an excellent four. They got into financial trouble, the fours costing more to make than they could earn, (a theme we'll see again and again) and the Hendersons sold out to Ignaz Schwinn, who was both a canny businessman and a motorcycle nut.

The Henderson was suitably rebadged and became the top of the Excelsior line; no pretense involved, by the way. They simply imposed a big "X"

on the Henderson emblem. And part of the deal was that the Henderson designers would be part of the package, so they could improve the machine and in due course that's what happened. The Henderson X, an 80-cubic-inch sidevalve inline four, did well in the market.

But the Henderson brothers didn't like some of Schwinn's changes and ideas—just like the buyouts of today with some soap opera thrown in—so they quit. Thomas Henderson went into a different business, but William Henderson designed another motorcycle using *his* new ideas, and raised money on the strength of his excellent reputation and returned to the two-wheeled wars. Since Schwinn owned the rights to the name of the Henderson motorcycle, Henderson called his new model the Ace.

The Ace got off to a good start. It was a sound design and machine and the market was there. But in 1922, Henderson was killed in a testing accident. Arthur Lemon, who'd worked as a designer for Henderson and stayed with Excelsior, resigned from that firm and returned to Henderson, um, Ace. He made even more improvements and things went well until the bookkeepers realized the cost of the bike was more than its selling price.

Meanwhile, the Hendee Manufacturing Company had been helping Ace with items such as engine

In 1929, with timing as unfortunate as it could have been, Indian brought out the first all-Indian Four, a mix of Ace engine and Indian running gear. Jeff Hackett

The photogenic side of the Indian Ace featured a row of exhaust pipes, so there was no doubt as to how many cylinders the machine had, which gave status and power then as now. *Jeff Hackett*

castings, so when Ace stopped production and distributed its various assets, the managers at Indian bought the manufacturing rights to the Ace, and an Indian Ace was shown at the 1927 Motorcycle Show in New York. Again, there was no subterfuge here; if the makers had been tempted to fudge, surely the knowledgeable riders of the day would have shown them up.

The Indian Four was introduced as the Indian Ace, subtitled the Collegiate Four. It was much more

Ace than Indian, with right-hand throttle and left-hand shift, and with leading link (as in H-D style) forks. The engine was intake-over-exhaust, inline, 77ci. Wheelbase was 59 inches, and the claimed weight was 395 pounds. Indian had designed and marketed the Ace as a sporting four, which is why it had the collegiate label, as college sports then were what professional sports, as in football and tennis, are now. And Ace engines had been used in special

frames for hill climbs and had run endurance contests in stock frames and done well.

This is a wonderful example of one hand/other hand history. On the one hand, the Henderson brothers were the hands, sorry, behind both what became the Excelsior and the Indian fours. On the other hand, the idea of the four-cylinder motorcycle had such appeal that some really good engineers spent time and talent improving on what the Hendersons did. It wasn't long, 18 months or so, before the Indian Ace was replaced by the Indian Four, model number 401, which in essence was the Ace engine and gearbox in a frame that looked like the all-new and radically suc-

cessful 101 Scout but used heavier tubes. The front suspension was normal Indian leaf spring; It's not difficult to imagine the Indian crew wincing every time they looked at those leading links of the former Ace.

So, the Indian Four is part of the family and the saga. What about H-D?

Harley and the Davidsons had been paying close attention. More than that, in fact. There was still another struggling maker of a four named Cleveland. The owners of the brand, which wasn't doing any better than the other fours had done, offered to sell out, which would have made H-D the third of the three majors to absorb a four-cylinder into its catalog.

The founders thought about it. They got hold of a Cleveland and took it to pieces. Unfortunately, the records here aren't as complete as historians might like, but the design seems to have been better than the execution, or the intentions were better than the design. Whichever, the engineers examined and reported and H-D's directors, that is, the four founders, decided not buy the plant or the design.

Meanwhile, Cleveland failed, Excelsior shut down with the Depression, Harley-Davidson didn't build a rival four, and we'll see the Indian Four later. It did lend prestige to the make, even if it didn't make much difference.

It's new model time (1928), and Hap Alzina, on the left, has come to the Indian factory in Springfield to pick up his 401, the first really Indian Four. The other guys are Indian execs and appear to be out for just a spin, witness their overcoats and ties. But Alzina is ready for the road in his pioneer-era rain suit and gauntlet gloves. . . . except he hasn't swapped his railroad-travel shoes for boots to go with the rain suit. Hap Alzina Archives

The left side of the early fours wasn't as photogenic, with the electrics just sort of bolted on. The kick start is on the left because that was the most convenient way to access the primary drive.

The Ace, designed and built by Henderson after the Henderson brand was owned by Excelsior. This was an excellent machine that made use of improvements the first models and subsequent owner of the make hadn't thought of. Note the wheelbarrow handlebars and the tank in the frame rails. The clutch pedal and gearshift lever were on the left, one of the several things Indian changed when they took over Ace. *Roy Kidney*

The Indian Ace in the foreground and the Indian 401 behind were alike and different at the same time. Indian struck, so to speak, just as the iron cooled off. *Jeff Hackett*

Chapter Ten

The 101 Scout and the Model D

Advantage, Indian

Just how Indian came up with the 101 Scout, arguably its best model ever and more clearly still the best motorcycle for its class and time, has never been explained. Instead, all the official histories make it so clear that when this took place in the late 1920s, Indian was in such deep trouble that just making any motorcycle tested the laws of nature and economics.

Begin with Indian's owners caring only about playing with and in the stock market and with the factory's space and equipment entangled in poorly planned schemes to build outboard motors and refrigerators. Add in the new Indian Ace/Four, the successful Chief and Big Chief, the exportable Prince, the racing team and its overhead valve factory fliers, and not at all least, the Scout 45, which was selling as fast as they could bolt 'em together.

In March 1928, with the motorcycles doing well and the company doing poorly, Indian introduced a new and improved Scout, to use a phrase the ad guys would do to death later. They did so with a technique later perfected by Harley-Davidson, that of leap-frogging improvements so the new doesn't overwhelm the improved.

In this example, the Scout 45 was a proven engine and drivetrain. The first version, the 37-cubic-inch Scout, had worked fine and did even bet-ter when it was made larger. The bugs and weak spots were taken care of by 1928.

Indian's engineers took this excellent engine and gearbox and put it into a new frame. It was a better frame, stiffer, and made of the best steel they could use, with a 2 1/2-longer wheelbase, nominal—the wheelbase varies when you adjust the chain—57 1/8 inches.

Some of the extra room was used to give the battery a permanent home, because lights, generator, and battery were standard by this time. And part of the extra length may have been to make the bike more stable at high speeds. In that department, the fork rake was kicked out some, which also makes a motorcycle steer straighter and more surely. The factory said the new settings came from racing, and they probably did.

The gas and oil tanks were shorter and more streamlined. Perhaps the most obvious and easiest to sell feature was the seat, which was three inches lower than on the first Scout and gave a static ride height of only 26 1/4 inches with an "average rider" aboard.

Designer Franklin also took advantage of the major changes to make some less visible fixes. The first Scouts used plates that bolted to the engine and then to the frame, for instance, except that the col-

The 101 Scout was basically the original, improved. It had a stronger frame, improved steering and suspension, the proven 45-cubic-inch engine, and, of course, the radical new front brake. This example is a daily driver, which explains the mirror and non-stock horn. *Roy Kidney*

Indian's stylists had developed a family heritage by 1928, and the 101 looks new and like the earlier Prince at the same time. Jeff Hackett

lection of pieces flexed and broke. The 101 Scout's cases were extended, and the mounting bosses were part of the engine, attached to the frame lugs with through bolts. The frame stiffened the engine, the engine did the same for the frame, and the breakage was no more.

There are lots of deft touches in this model. There's a bracket below the seat that most obviously is where the seat mounts. But look more closely, and the bracket also locates the rear fender, and because the mounting holes are slotted, the belt driving the generator can be kept in correct tension.

There's also a knob and control rod located within easy reach of the rider, jutting from the fuel tank. The control is routed through a tunnel in the tank, and it opens the exhaust valves, which releases compression and stops the engine.

Why all this? Because electricity was still suspect in 1928, not without cause, and the notion was that shorting out an operating magneto was bad for it, while lifting the exhaust valves was simply a mechanical operation. It's kind of like the electronic

black boxes 60 years later except that in the present time, you *can* hurt the system if it fires sparks with no place to dissipate.

A Bike of Many Parts

One of the basic yarns from the past claims things were easier back then. Interviews with Indian fanciers frequently turn up the notion that one of Indian's strengths was its simplicity. This causes guys who work on them to fall on the shop floor, laughing. Restorer Jerry Greer points out that a Scout engine has 108 bearing rollers, 48 in the connecting rod's big end alone. Each of these rollers must be exactly sized, by hand, on rebuild.

The various bearings, bushings, and shafts are replaceable, at least, and come in stair step sizes, so a cylinder can be rebored several times, with a slightly larger piston being used each time. The engine itself will thus last indefinitely, barring blow-up but sometimes even then. Thing is, the designs were done when time was a cheaper component than it is now..

George Yarocki, president of the 101 Club, reinforces the non-simple claim with a basic statistic: the 101 Scout is assembled of 4,000 parts. Remember the multiple-purpose seat bracket? The seat and its mounting system alone are comprised of 116 separate parts. Yarocki suspects this was done so when some bit fell off, which happened, the owner would buy a new assembly instead of tracking down the washers, brackets, or whatever.

About the Name

The 101 Scout is the only production Indian referred to in public, as opposed to factory or dealer codes, with a number. The official record never bothered to state why that happened. My best guess is that it was an accident. The 101 Scout simply appeared as that in the ads, and the numbers stuck. But the Prince, the single cylinder basic bike, was referred to as the 201. And the first Indian-framed four, the model that quickly replaced the Indian Ace, was designated the 401.

Indian seems to have been adopting a new code, replacing the earlier letters with series numbers. The numbers in turn came at random, so the one-cylinder model was the 200 series, the Chief twin was the 300 line, the four lucked into 400, and the Scout—could it have been the engine they began the series with?—was the 101.

Next, the factory added model year numbers, which made the 1933 Chief the 333, and so forth. Indian used this code for the next decade at least. But the public didn't. Instead, they used those easy names: the Prince, Scout, and Chief. The major variation was with the Scout, as in the Police Special, Short Frame, or later Sport Scout. The exception, the Scout with no nickname, was the 101. And so it is to this day.

Not Quite a Contest

Indian's timing couldn't have been better. The 101 Scout appeared in the spring of 1928. The Harley-Davidson 45, the Model D, went into production in July of that same year. So H-D hit the market with a model aimed at the Indian 45, which Indian had just improved upon. Not only that, there were problems with the early Ds, so the production line didn't move as fast as the sales came in, putting Harley's middleweight at a disadvantage right away.

That wasn't the worst part. There were no tests being done than in the manner invented later. Each ad department was free to puff and extol as they pleased, while the riding public could brag and judge and condemn for themselves.

The two models, the 101 and the D and stage-one-tuned DL, were nearly as similar as two 1928 45-cubic-inch motorcycles could have been. Both had a front brake, front suspension, rigid rear wheel, hand-shift, foot clutch, headlight as part of the package, kick start, three forward speeds, and so forth.

The DL had a wheelbase of 56 1/2 inches, the 101's was 57 1/8. The Harley's bore and stroke were 2 3/4x3 13/16, the Indian's were 2 7/8x3 1/2. The 101 weighed 370 to 385 pounds, the Harley a few pounds more; there were no official weights at the time, but because the Harley 45 was originally drawn up as a 37-cubic-inch engine, the frame was light so the DL and the 101 were surely close in weight.

In actual performance, a subject to be detailed as official results enter the picture, folklore and rider recall give the edge to the Indian. Inside guesses rated the 101 engine at 20 horsepower, which the Harley couldn't match. Just as important, the 101 didn't break down, having been debugged for eight years, while the D and DL needed corrections.

The major factor, though, was intangible. Designer Franklin began as a racer, and he must have had a feel for a good machine, reinforced by experience and formal training. While the financial and management people were doing harm, Franklin was allowed to do good.

Somehow, in ways that can't be discerned 60-plus years later, the 101 Scout felt right. It balanced and steered and responded better than the bigger bikes or the rival 45s. Guys who rode them then still get misty eyes when they talk about what the 101 would do, to the extent that a surprising number of the riders then are 101 riders now, witness the rival clubs in 1996, 65 years after the 101 went out of production.

The new 101 Scout was longer and lower, partially because of the new frame and partially because the front end had more rake to keep the machine stable at speed. Static ride height was listed as 25 inches. George and Millie Yarocki

*N*aturally, the 101 Scout is clearly at home on the range. This 1930 example has been equipped with a luggage rack and seat cover, the better to travel the open road. *Jeff Hackett*

The sad how and why of the 101's demise began before production did, back when the new owners diversified. When Harley-Davidson's production stumbled, when the orders for 101s flooded in, the factory had been occupied by the small car project. Indian had become a manufacturing company.

They did what they could. The smaller Chief, the 61, was dropped from the line-up in 1928, and 101 production at one point reached 75 a day, not bad for those days. But first, because the plant was being wasted, despite the demand for motorcycles, in 1928 Indian only made 5,000 machines. And Indian lost money, piles of it.

If that happened during the good times, what about the bad times, which now were looming?

Cracking the Code

The identification systems used by Indian and Harley-Davidson through their histories recall the joke about the Theory of Relativity: only two people

have ever understood it, one is dead and the other has forgotten the details.

H-D began with plain numbers. Because 1908 was the fourth year of production, that year's machines were called the Model 4. Letters were used to identify equipment, as in the Model 5 with battery, 5A with optional magneto ignition. When the twin arrived, the letters designated the engine, C for a single, D or E for the twin. In 1916 the numbers became calendar year, as in 16B or 16F, until the numbers

were assumed and the models known, with the exception of the Sport Twin, as the J or JD or whatever.

Up front, Indian made it easy by using names, as in Chief, Scout, Powerplus, and so on. In detail, Indian's system was much more complicated. Very early examples were simply numbered as they came off the production line. Then the twins got a T (which makes sense) and the singles an H, for reasons known only to Indian. Then came more letters and engine numbers, which began with 101 instead of 001 after 1921.

The 101 Scout is one Indian with a left side as tidy and attractive as the right. All-gear primary was efficient and expensive. *Jeff Hackett*

87

Later, the named models received code numbers. The larger models make sense, as in the Four was the 401 and the Chief was the 301, but the lower numbers didn't, with the little single as 201 and the twin-cylinder Scout was the 101. The final system was to combine the model number with the year, making the 1940 Chief the 340 but the 1940 Scout was the 640. Go figure.

Worse, the factory kept the books for itself. Not until the government required details, numbers, and procedures as part of the bid for military contracts did the Indian owners learn the official way to service and repair. (The material from the war has served countless restorers since, in one of that rarest of events, the man from the government who really did help.)

Harley-Davidson used a logic that followed the fact. There were no Harley names until just before the close of this history. Instead, letters designated engines, then equipment. The intake-over-exhaust twins were D, E, F, and J, with other letters added as needed. The J was the 61-cubic-inch version, the JD was the 74, H was added with the 2-cam lower end, L was for the sporting model, and so

forth. It seems the drafting department liked some letters better than others and assigned them on what looks now like a whimsical basis.

D has been used for two series of engines, likewise E, F, and W. X holds the record with three engines: the 1912 single with clutch, the World War II shaft-drive twin, and the 1957-current Sportster. But D for Davidson was okay and H has never been used for an engine. Instead, H has meant two cams with the J engines, more displacement with the VL and K, and a stronger lower end with the FL.

And there are contradictions, as in the tuned version of the D-series twin was the DL, but the tuned K was the KK. In the late 1970s, H-D finally used letters as abbreviations, as in the XLT for touring, with thick seat and larger tank, and the FXR for rubber mount. But they went so far, as in FXDWG, meaning F for the engine series, X for the Sportster-style front end, D for the Daytona (rubber-mount) chassis, and WG for Wide Glide forks, that the riders ignore the whole thing.

You can learn the code. What you can't do is crack it.

*T*op of the line for 1934, the VLD is so called because of V for the side-valve 74-cubic-inch engine, L for the higher compression, and D for the sport package. *Jeff Hackett*

Chapter Eleven

Indian on the Brink

The Best of Men, the Worst of Times

Family wealth and really good genes notwithstanding, when he was a kid, E. Paul du Pont liked reading boy's adventure magazines, the ones with the derring-do in front and the neat ads in the back. Back when Paul du Pont was a kid, just after the turn of the century, these ads included kits, with which you could bolt an internal combustion engine onto a bicycle and have speed beyond your wildest dreams.

Paul and his brother came up with the money and learned they'd been had. What they got was some parts that needed work and some plans that didn't explain what they needed to know. But they were not without resources, their family having become a household word and several name brands on the basis of intelligence, creativity, and hard work.

Back then, industrial powerhouses were different and the du Pont family lived right next to the actual plant in Delaware. The brothers had access to the machine shop, and they knew how to operate the equipment—they were in their early teens at this point—and they did all they knew how to do. No go. Literally. In other words, they pedaled around and around the back yard, but the engine wouldn't fire.

Because home and factory were so close, their father knew what they were doing and how hard they were working. Du Pont Sr. wasn't a mechanical engineer; he was a chemist. He ducked into his lab and brewed some special fuel, leaning heavily on ether, his grandkids guessed two generations later. The kit engine ran, not very well, but at least they had the pleasure of hearing their work in action.

Their industry had impressed dad. This was how all fathers hope their sons will turn out, after all. du Pont Sr. knew nothing about motorcycles, which were then in their infancy, but he knew the local Packard dealer and he knew the Packard man knew machines, so he asked the dealer what brand motorcycle was best. Right. Indian. Thus, in his formative years, E. Paul du Pont became a motorcycle enthusiast and an Indian owner.

Fast-forward 20 years: Paul du Pont becomes an engineer, files for and is awarded nearly a dozen patents, and goes into the motorcar business, making DuPonts (note that the family is du Pont, while the company is DuPont). By all accounts they were good cars, even though they didn't make the family any richer.

Pual du Pont was also what's now known as a private investor. At this time, the 1920s, Indian's owners and managers were using their holdings to invest in, OK play, the stock market. To make a long

E. Paul du Pont, astride the Indian single donated to the Smithsonian Institution and still on display there. According to family and factory records, it's a 1901 model. Some restorers have said it's a 1903 or later, but the du Pont's say they fitted later wheels back in the teens. *The du Pont family*

This happy couple doesn't look like they're out of work, but this ad has obviously been pitched toward motorcyclists who are feeling the pinch. The ad ran in *Popular Mechanics* magazine. It assumes the reader wants a motorcycle and is troubled only by the cost. Oh, and the machine is a VL, a big twin, while the price quote applies to the new (and much cheaper) Single.

Harley-Davidson's new big twin, the 74-cubic-inch V series, was sidevalve rather than intake-over-exhaust, which followed Indian's lead and dismayed the H-D faithful. Even worse, the first examples off the production line had lots of problems. But because the V was, as it looks here, a large and sturdy design that worked on the open road or in the police department, the new model was accepted and it kept the production line, well, producing.

and complicated story as short as possible, Paul du Pont had done all he wanted to do with cars, he had money to invest and (again, according to family history) he liked motorcycles *and* Indian must have looked like a good company in the wrong hands.

When the flurry of dealing was over, the DuPont car company had become part of Indian, and Indian was under the control of E. Paul du Pont. This happened, as they said in the boy's adventure magazines of that day and this, in the nick of time. As soon as he got an inside look at the operations and the books, du Pont knew he had to take action. This was early in 1930, the business of motorcycling was becoming almost purely a sport, the world's economies were sliding into disaster, and some truly shabby managers were looting Indian for all that was left.

Paul du Pont dispatched his trusted lieutenants, Joe Hosley and Allan Carter, to see what was going on, and make it stop, which they did. The details have faded, but one of the reasons du Pont was

able to take control seems to have been that he had the goods on the bad guys.

How the Times Changed

Some of the action of du Pont and his lieutenants was simple, as in making the people stop taking stuff they had no right to take. Some of the action was just as basic, in that they had to figure out what they had left in the plant and what they should do with it. And some of what du Pont and his staff had to do—at this point one can imagine them heaving a sigh of relief—had to do with motorcycles.

The change from Roaring Twenties to Depressed Thirties needs no documentation here, except to note that people obviously had less money to spend on anything, food and shelter even. For our purposes, again noting the obvious, this hurt motorcycling. Beyond that, though, the transition was complete. Back in the early days, the motorcycle competed with the car (and to some degree the bicycle and the trolley) in the contest as to what would be true mass transit, as in what would move most people most places, when they had a choice.

The car won. Cars were what everybody wanted, and lots of people had and liked them and didn't even think about the horse, bicycle, trolley, or bus. As a result, motorcycle companies died. Cleveland, which had never been very strong, formally folded. Excelsior, whose owner liked motorcycles but knew his son wasn't as keen, had been in business to the extent his products kept the other two firms

alert. But when the economy collapsed, Schwinn did the sensible thing and shut down for good.

One against one is the best sort of feud. Emphasizing this was the change from transportation. OK, hardly anybody has ever ridden a motorcycle because it's cheap. That's what we tell our moms, but it's not so, and probably never was. Except that back in the teens, the ads suggested a motorcycle could get you home for hot lunch. And in 1930, there was an H-D ad that said "Only a sportsman appreciates a motorcycle. No box of wood and glass for him." Change the word "box" to the word "cage" and you have the biker slogan from then until right this minute.

Not the least reason for this shift from what you can do with a motorcycle to what she'll do for you, was that racing had become a spectacle, and the machines so specialized that they shared the number of wheels and not much else. There were deaths and crashes and the public reckoned all riders and bikers to be thrill-crazed loonies, and they were treated as such more often than not.

One final factor has to have been family life. Consider that most young men couldn't afford to get married or have homes of their own, not back then. And there was no television, home videos, computer games, or any of the myriad devices that now keep the generations out of each other's hair.

Skeptics may wish to look this up, but the record shows there was much more peer socializing, with men's lodges, women's clubs, and ethnic and profession groups, than there is now. There were no condos or bachelor pads and young men did not sit home playing cards with their moms or reading good books—and don't let your grandma tell you otherwise.

Where all this led to was the motorcycle club. There had been such clubs since the bicycle days. Riders of whatever brand, mostly men and mostly young but not always, got together on the weekends, rode places, and did events. But with the decline in motorcycle sales and use, with there being not much else to do, and with the stratification of those in the sport and the vast majority not, the motorcycle club

became the place bike nuts went at night and during the weekend. They had club houses, with pool tables and kitchens and places to make coffee and snacks and not least have a beer.

Put all this together and we get parallel history. The motorcycle nearly dies, and the Harley-Indian feud becomes the stuff of legend and, in a few examples, leads to genuine fights. What history has neglected until now, though, is that if it hadn't been for Paul du Pont, the Harley guys almost surely wouldn't have had anybody to feud with.

When the Going Got Tough

Timing is everything, a book for new husbands in the Victorian Era is supposed to have said, and the theory fits motorcycles as well as it does women, for better and for worse. The better timing belonged, at the onset of the Great Depression, to Harley-Davidson. The founders had been aware that their products weren't up to date, and they'd planned accordingly. The D series of 45s, the middleweights, had been the first part of the update, and while they weren't as good as the Scouts, they kept Milwaukee in contention.

A better move—and a freak of lucky timing—was the new line of heavyweights, the 74-cubic-inch V series. Why the freak part? Because the V series had some serious problems. The design itself was not

Counter to conventional wisdom, when the V series was introduced as 1930 models, the big bike was fitted with the four-pipe mufflers and small dual headlights used at the end of the intake-over-exhaust J series production, making the new ones look older than they were. © Harley-Davidson Motor Company

This bike is something of a mystery. Remember H-D's DAH engine, the overhead valve 750 made to compete with the similar engines from Indian and Excelsior, the racing engine never sold for the street? This photo was taken in the early 1930s at the Harley plant. It looks like a DAH engine in a road-going frame, with dropped handlebars, a tool box, a rear wheel stand, and four straight pipes— an odd mix. The official version has for years been that this machine was built for road racing in Europe. But there were no classes for 750s in Europe then. Some people (mostly the author of this book) suspect this was an experiment, to see how an overhead valve 750 would work on the road, as compared with the sidevalve big twins and the Sport Scout coming from Indian. ©
Harley-Davidson Motor Company

merely conventional, it clearly followed Indian's side-valve engine theme after nearly 25 years of using the intake-over-exhaust design. The V series retained the separate engine bolted into the frame and the gearbox ditto, sliding back and forth to adjust the primary chain's tension, along with rigid rear wheel and the leading-link forks.

Just about all the parts, though, were new: frame, engine, forks, and most of the bolt-on bits, excepting odd items like spark plugs, a few bearings, and the occasional piece of rubber. There was the plain V, the higher-compression VL, and the choice of magneto ignition, which added an M to the other two letters.

The Vs may be why H-D has been careful ever since not to change the engine and the cycle parts at the same time. Things went wrong at first. Wheels were weak and came loose, the clutch didn't feel right, starting and timing were difficult to learn, the flywheels were too light, and the engine bucked at low speed. It was a long list, so long that production stopped while the engineers corrected things.

The timing was bad, in that the troubles were very public. A lot of JD and JDH owners felt betrayed by Harley going the sidevalve route as per Indian, and they took pleasure in watching the new models collapse. This gave rise to stories still circulating, if you find the right crowd of veterans, about how the JDH would outrun and outlast the V and VL.

Historian Hatfield took the trouble to research this legend and was told by the late Tom Sifton, tuner and dealer, that it plain wasn't so. When the teething problems were handled, which they were, the VL would handily outrun the JDH, especially on long top-speed pulls, which caused the older bikes to melt down. The V design was stout, with a claimed weight of 529 pounds and a wheelbase of 60 inches. This was bigger than the 45s from either brand, as it should have been. The factory estimated top speed of 85 for the VL, 80 for the plain V.

The timing becomes good simply because just when the new models were found faulty and production had to stop, the Depression really hit. Wall

Street's collapse wasn't a fluke, as the farmers who'd overworked their land and the politicians who'd imposed foolish tariffs added to the economy's troubles. And nobody was buying motorcycles.

Life takes odd turns, eh? While they weren't being pressured by demands from the buying public, Harley's designers and managers had the time and the resources to make the improvements. At the same time, they redid the 45, into the R series, with the generator horizontal instead of vertical, with internal improvements, and with a better frame.

How Harley-Davidson worked at its best is shown by the time Sifton arrived to pick up the first new 45. He mentioned a frame improvement he made to the older series, and before he headed for home, Sifton's improvement had been incorporated on the production bikes, at the instruction of William Harley, the chief engineer. Sometimes Not Invented Here didn't matter.

The bad, or perhaps unlucky, timing took place at Springfield. It's almost beyond irony to note that in 1928 and 1929, when the red ink went

During the depth of the Depression, police business was nearly the only business. This rig, with armor plate for operator and passenger and with ports through which they can return fire, surely was intended for counter-rumrunner duty. *Hap Alzina Archives*

beyond one million dollars, Indians won every national championship event. So much for the stock car slogan Win on Sunday, sell on Monday. That combination of racing success and sales failure caused du Pont to view the role of management as sort of a receiver, as in, don't spend any money that can be saved. All the non-motor projects, the small car, the outboard motor, and the automotive shock absorbers were abandoned: Not having them was cheaper than losing money on every sale.

The major change, in terms of history, was that the 101 Scout was removed from the line-up. There are those who are still resentful of this, nearly 70 years later. And it does seem strange, in that the 101s were selling faster than the factory could make them. But the records show the 101 was as expensive to make as the Chief was, and one of the firmer facts in the motoring industry is that you can't sell small vehicles for as much as large ones, no matter that the small ones cost as much to make. This has to have been especially true here, because Harley-Davidson

was ready to match the Chief with the new VL, dollar for dollar, and had its 45 twins in the same class as the 101. OK, the Scout was faster, but it wasn't as fast as a 74, so it had to sell for less.

Here's the timing problem. Indian had no money, in fact the payroll was met several times by Hap Alzina, the west coast distributor who showed up with satchels of cash, and later by loans from the neighborhood bank. Things were that tight.

In the face of that, Indian came out with the Standard Scout, basically the 101 engine installed in the Chief frame. The Standard Scout weighed at least 80 pounds more than the 101 had, and it was slower and less sporty, which hurt in the sales department, but it did save money; and the ads made it clear that when things got better, the Standard Scout owner could buy and easily install the full 74 Chief engine.

Next, bolder than brass, Indian invented the Hot Rod Cycle. Not that they called it that. But the frame design and girder front forks of the Prince single were revived, and into the lightweight chassis was stuffed a modified Scout 101 engine. They called it Motoplane and in case the punchline was obscure, the ads showed fighter planes zooming through the sky.

Just in case that was too much (as it proved to be), there was a less extreme version, a destroked 101 engine, displacing 30.50 cubic inches or 500cc, installed in the same light frame with girder forks. It was called the Pony Scout at first, later the Junior Scout, and the idea was, the 500cc engine was more controllable than the 750 so it was Indian's entry level machine, not that the term was used then.

There were some internal concerns, in that Franklin was in poor health. He went on leave in 1931 and died the next year. DuPont's manager from the car company, Joe Hosley, had taken over the same job at Indian, and for a time he was acting chief engineer, as the engineering department fell under his jurisdiction. Then Indian took on a racer and technical wizard named Jimmy Hill who provided the much-needed new ideas.

Perhaps the major improvement across the line was conversion of Indian's engines to a better oiling system. This sounds more obvious than it was. When the internal combustion engine was being invented, gas and oil were simply fed to it and consumed. Gas went to the carb, oil to the sump. When they were used, you pumped in more. Because the oil, like the fuel, was used once, the system was known as total loss, which implies to us now that the oil was run through the engine and dumped out, which it wasn't.

Cars and their engines were much bigger than motorcycles, and car engines got away from this right away by putting the oil in a pan beneath the crankcase, a system known as wet sump. Racing cars, though, needed lots of oil and low centers of gravity, so they often had dual oil pumps and a separate oil tank, with the pump delivering oil to the engine and then returning it to the tank.

That was known as dry sump, and that's what Indians got in 1933. (Harley-Davidson made two moves in response: First, it said that Harley engines only got new, clean, fresh oil, unlike some engines,

and second, four years later, it converted Harley engines to dry sump, which they still are.)

Another general improvement was sort of a family move. Paul du Pont's family was of course deeply involved in the paint business, and he called on his cousins or uncles or whoever, and got the family deal on paint. There were 24 or so basic colors and combinations offered in 1934, this when the Harley catalog showed one or two. If DuPont made a shade of paint, you could get that shade on your new Indian.

These moves were good ones for the most part. The only technical problem turned out to be that the Motoplane had more power than its lightweight frame could contain and things flexed, broke, and fell off. In the vast scheme of things, this wasn't much of a problem. Only a handful, make that several hundred, Motoplanes were sold and the model was replaced as soon as it could be done. But first, the failure of the design had to have discouraged the faithful few who'd bought them, and second but not least, Indian had invested money it didn't have in making changes that didn't work. Indian really needed to sell motorcycles at a time when nobody was buying. Bad timing, in sum, as well as unlucky.

A Few Good Moves

The paint choices and the dry sump oiling were good moves. Paul du Pont also paid a lot of attention to engineering problems that had been neglected. For instance, Indian fanciers liked to say that riding a Harley was like taking a long hike, the point being that the Harley shook so much your feet roamed up and down on the floorboards. (OK, so it's funnier in person than in print.) And the JD guys as well as the Indian tribe said the VLs were weak.

But the Indian files have du Pont himself riding the Chief and reporting to his staff that it vibrated so badly he had trouble hanging on, plus it was worse, on his experience, than the Harley 74. These guys weren't fools, and they sampled each other's products just as the car companies have

It's Saturday morning in front of the clubhouse and the guys are nearly ready to take off. Judging from the bedrolls strapped to the handlebars, it's an overnight run. And this club wasn't just for one make: that's an Indian third from the left. Jerry Greer

There are several trends here. This photo was taken in the 1930s while the first bike in line is a J series Harley, not new. Then comes a first-year VL and another intake-over-exhaust, both with special paint; then a really old, flatside tank J model. And the first in line has bobbed his rear fender, all of which shows that you rode what you could buy or build, and that the building had already begun. Jerry Greer

always bought samples of their competition for comparison and yes, duplicatory, purposes.

The Indian files also contain letters from dealers disturbed because the Chiefs didn't hold up under hard use, making them unfit for police duty, this at a time when police departments were the domestic motorcycle makers' best customers. We're aware and we're working on it, du Pont assured the dealers, and before you could say, "License and registration, please," the Chief engine had new flywheels and less vibration.

Corporate Connections

One of motorcycling's main survival factors began with what can be called an unhappy accident. All sports need some sort of referee, some impartial body willing to hold the coats and enforce the rules.

Maybe two days after the first two riders engaged in a contest of speed, such a body was created for motorcycle racing. There were several such groups during the course of early history, but by the time the Depression arrived, *the* national club was the American Motorcycle Association. The AMA laid down the rules, enforced the rules and records, and paid its own way with dues and fees. All to the good.

Then nobody could afford to buy motorcycles or pay dues and racing had become a circus. There were fewer than 100,000 motorcycles registered for road use in the United States. Only a tiny fraction of the owners and riders cared to go racing, so most didn't pay dues and the AMA was on the edge of disappearance.

The local clubs, the makers of parts and accessories, the racing promoters and track owners, and the men at the three surviving factories knew the AMA had to survive. The concerned parties met, negotiated, and agreed, the AMA would be supported by the trade, meaning mostly the factories.

This wasn't exactly made public. Various rule and regulation changes and classes of memberships were drawn up. Riders still paid dues. But in fact, the factories were paying the piper and we know what that means even if, as happened here, the rules of fair play weren't stretched very far very often.

I mention this cooperation here and now because it raises another sheet of unwashed laundry: the true (but less publicized) fact that after Excelsior had suspended operation, the executives and owners of H-D and Indian met with each other on a regular basis, to talk about business and who-knows-what.

Accounts have been published asserting that these meetings were illegal and that the two sides often clashed at them. These accounts conclude that the feud between Harley-Davidson and Indian began at the top.

Two Sides of the Tracks

The record, more carefully examined, indicates otherwise. What there seems to have been, in terms of conflict, could best be described as a culture gap. Paul du Pont was from the east coast and the Ivy League—old money, as they say. And just because he could ride motorcycles and improve engines and take out patents on his ideas didn't mean he didn't seem to be what he was, a member of the upper class. That's not mentioned as criticism, simply fact.

Just as true, Harley and the Davidsons were from the Midwest, from families working as skilled craftsmen. Before the founders got into the motorcycle business, they worked for the railroad. This was at a time when grown men still settled questions with their fists, when the foreman was chosen at least in part because he could use might to make right. And the Davidsons, like 95 percent of the American people at the turn of the century, reckoned themselves fortunate to not have to go to work until after high school. College wasn't an option, never mind the Ivy League.

Add the fact that Walter Davidson was H-D's president, du Pont's opposite number. Walter Davidson was the firm's founding motorcycle nut, remember, the man who won that enduro with a perfect score back in '08. And he had the racing team under his wing. And Walter Davidson had a rough tongue. Interviews with those who knew the man take one of three views: 1) Davidson talked rough, you wouldn't want your wife, mother, or daughters in the room; 2) Davidson talked rough when it was just the guys in the shop. In public, in mixed company, he was as polite as anyone could ask for, and 3) Oh heck! Everybody used bad words then, politically correct hadn't been invented.

Allan Carter asserts that there was no feud, no insults or bad feelings or even much that was personal about competing for the same, dwindling, business. He was the man sent by du Pont to investigate the goings-on at the Indian plant, and he was a troubleshooter and aide to du Pont during the latter's tenure at Indian.

"A feud? The dealers made that up. Ill feelings didn't exist at the factory level." In fact, Carter says, Harley-Davidson gave Indian permission to make dual seats similar to the H-D version, and Indian's electrical parts, for example, the ignition switch and generator, used Harley designs. It worked the other way too, Carter recalls. "We swapped parts and ideas back and forth. And we got along very well."

Carter reminds us that the guys who reported such stories weren't actually in the room where the incidents did or didn't happen. As if to illustrate how amicable the relationship was, after du Pont sold his interest in Indian, Carter moved back to Wilmington, Delaware, DuPont headquarters, and opened a Harley-Davidson agency.

Proving what? Mostly proving that the president of Indian and the president of Harley-Davidson didn't always speak the same language.

They've got to where they were going—California's high desert from the look of the terrain—and now it's time to see how many guys can pile aboard one bike. Jerry Greer

Chapter Twelve

The Sport Scout and Model RLDR

Birth of Class C Racing

Just when motorcycling looked to be in as bad a spot as any sport can get, when it looked as if things couldn't get worse, things got better.

And while the sport's recovery wasn't exactly an accident, it's probably safe to say with hindsight that not even the guys who did it knew how good they were doing at the time. Nor did they expect, witness the poem below, that the rivalry between the two makes would become legend, and entertainment.

What they had in mind was survival. At Indian, President du Pont's in-house receivership was paying off, in that each year after 1929 saw the deficit reduced by half and then half of that. Harley and the Davidsons didn't need to go quite that far, as they had money in the bank, the plant was paid for, and they had a larger dealer network that hadn't been lumbered by stuff like outboard motors and car parts.

Even so, there was consideration given at H-D to simply getting out of the business, as Schwinn had done at Excelsior. Nor could they be blamed. Tradition is all very well, but Harley's founders had seen 200 firms go into the motorcycle business and 198 go out, some feet first. The founders had made money, they had families to support, and if they hadn't had faith that things would/could get better, they

could easily have voted to shut down the plant and look for something else to do.

But, as we all heave sighs of relief, they didn't. They voted to cut back and to carry on. By the happiest of accidents, Harley and Indian now had a controlling interest in the AMA, at a time when professional racing was nearly dead, and what there was, mostly short track or speedway, was outside the AMA's jurisdiction.

So the AMA created a new class of racing. It was what we'd now call production class, in that the machines were supposed to be stock, as they came from the showroom. The rules went so far in that direction that the riders were required to own the bikes and there was even an initial requirement that the bikes be ridden to the track and stripped of their road gear there, instead of being prepped at home and trailered to the track.

Here's one of the carefully worded parts. The new class, with exceptions to be noted, was for 750cc, or 45-cubic-inch sidevalve engines, stock or with options. They were picked because sporting riders were already using and riding them. There were not picked so the riders would have to buy before they could race. Note that in the margin someplace.

Here's the idea the AMA guys had in mind for the new Class C: Griff Cathkart's Harley-Davidson WL is licensed for the road, witness the license plate bolted to the rear fender, but the lights have been removed, and the front brake drum lacks shoes and linkage (flat-track rules forbade brakes until the late 1960s; you stopped by slewing the bike sideways). © Harley-Davidson Motor Company

This 1934 Sport Scout is a survivor; it wears dirt track tanks but has brakes front and back, meaning it's ready for road race duty in today's vintage class. Jeff Hackett

The major exception to the rule was that the first national titles would still be won in the Class A and Class B professional classes, in flat track and for hill climbs, with alcohol fuel and full-race engines allowed. There would be an open class, no displacement limit, for hill climbs and for the newly adopted TT races.

Almost as an incidental, the amateur class, run what ya rode in on, would include 500cc overhead valve engines along with the 750 sidevalves. This provision was made because it seemed fair, giving the sidevalve engines more displacement, and because there were a couple of guys riding imports, mostly from England, and letting them race what they rode seemed sportsmanlike. As it was. These exceptions are mentioned here because later people would say the imports had been picked on. They hadn't been.

The dumb part was that because there were classes A and B already, the new class was called Class C, which has to have hampered racing because first thing you think of is that Class C is, well, third class.

Sport Scout

This happened too quickly to have been a plot, but in 1934, the same year Class C began, Indian introduced a new model, which was both perfect for the class, and which became a legend equaling, maybe even exceeding, the legend of the 101 Scout.

The name was Sport Scout, another good choice in that department. The point of departure was the under-built Motoplane. Indian's designers knew the idea—the powerful engine in the light chassis—was good. What they did now was make the idea work.

Central was an improved 101 Scout engine (Indian and Harley have traditionally evolved designs, so they can be retrofitted and easily replaced). Same bore and stroke and included angle, but with improved porting and larger carb and alloy heads, more to reduce heat than increase compression. The engine used dry sump oiling, with battery ignition standard and magneto optional, and the new Scout shared the rigid primary case, semi-unit, they said then, and the three-speed gearbox, with the Chief.

The frame was unique, in that there were two pieces, front and rear. At the top, they bolted together, while at the bottom, the engine bridged a gap. It wasn't a diamond, nor was it a keystone frame. But it was strong, albeit not as light as the Monoplane/Prince frame, and it worked.

Front suspension followed the same path, with the girder design from the earlier models but stronger and made of heavier metal. It also had a handshift, foot clutch, brakes on both ends, and a rigidly mounted rear wheel of course.

The other figures are tricky. Factories have never been famous for accuracy, plus there are shipping weights that are for dry machines and curbside weights with tanks topped, plus the bike stripped of lights, muffler brakes, and battery would weight less than when ready for the road.

A bit later in this period, Indian issued some official numbers. In 1936 the out-the-door Pony Scout weighed an official 340 pounds; the Sport Scout 420, the Scout 45 (that's the 45 engine in the Chief frame) 445, and the Chief 480.

Indian had a choice of tune, sort of a sliding scale. The first step up was the B version, the equivalent of Harley's L, but in 1935 the slightly higher compression ratio and larger intake of the B became the standard and the Y specifications, heavy-duty cylinders (don't forget that the ports were in the barrels, so tuned cylinders then were like the flowed and ported heads of today) and higher compression alloy heads, were the new option, priced at $9 for the Chief and $7.50 for the Sport and Standard Scouts. And when the factory talked about that, they said the race-ready Sport Scout weighed 310 pounds and had 41 horsepower, which it may well have done.

Model RLDR:
Harley's Counterpunch

The Indian with that much power came later. It has to have, because the record is too equal. Or the reverse. In 1934, when the Class C rules became

operable, most sport riders didn't have new bikes, nor were there that may events. In 1935, at the low point of motorcycle racing, only Harley had a factory team, and that was one man, Joe Petrali, who'd been hired when Excelsior shut down. In the 1935 season Petrali won all the national titles—yes, all of them. Now *there* is a record that will never be equaled.

The other word of course is borrrring. Petrali did it aboard the full-race single and the overhead valve racing twins, 45 or 61 depending on the events. Harley's production racer was the RLDR, R for the production 45 with horizontal generator, D and L for higher compression ratio and big carb, R for loose clearances. Less friction means more speed, even if you have to overhaul the engine more often. Factory figures show that engine with 30 horsepower and change, and because the machines were similar in wheelbase, weight, and design and because the Indians didn't clean the Harley clocks every time, we can assume the early Class C engines were both close to 30 horsepower, with Indian seeming to have an edge in speed and weight and with Harley having more riders because they sold more bikes.

This is obviously a desert or cross country race of some sort and the rider, Paul Derkum according to an educated guess, is handing back the water jug, his Sport Scout having been refueled. This type of event was rare by the mid-1930s, the open road having been taken into police custody. *Hap Alzina Archives*

This is Armando Magri, on his way to winning the 50-mile national TT at San Pedro, California, 1938. When TT racing was done on natural terrain, the organizers liked to have real hills to climb and jumps on which to get air. Armando Magri

Now, the fun begins. From this period, we find items like:

> "You'll never wear out
> The Indian Scout,
> or its brother,
> The Indian Chief.
> They're built like rocks
> To take hard knocks.
> It's the Harleys
> That cause the grief."

TT jumps were often big, and so were the bikes. As you can see here, when one racer goes down he makes it that much more difficult for the guys behind to get past. In this case, spectators are coming to help, except for the man at top right who is taking notes. Max Bubeck

Read that out loud three times and if you can remember your own phone number, you'll never forget that poem.

Earlier, the racers began having fun with the laughing Indian logo. And the makes were always competing on the track, the showroom, and the open road. But now, the few people who wanted to ride motorcycles were sports, and they had races to ride in as well as to ride to. They had clubhouses and they hung out together. And they chose up sides.

There were some geographic influences here, in that in a really small town, if three guys had bikes— two Harleys and one Indian, say—they'd still ride together on Sundays. But if there were two agencies in the area, like as not there'd be two clubs, and when they rode to the races they'd sit on different sides of the track. Or they'd get into punch-ups, which did happen.

More often, though, it was just good-hearted joking. Indian dealer Erwin Smith, who now runs a repair shop in Illinois, conceals a grin:

"Seems there was this Harley factory rep who took a shortcut down a dirt road and hit a rooster.

"He stopped and told the farmer, who was furious, said that was his best rooster and so forth.

"The Harley rep defended himself, said he was riding his Harley down the road and the rooster jumped out in front of him.

"The farmer stopped. 'A Harley? Well, if that dumb bird couldn't out-run a Harley, he ought to be dead.'"

Rim shot. Pause for belly laugh.

Yes, the joke can be turned around. Nothing prevents it. Except that by this time, 1935 or so, Harley had the sales lead and was the dominant force on the still-small market and as always seems to happen, the underdog attracted the guys who made better jokes, songs, poems, and so forth.

As in?

Why are Harleys painted green?

So they can hide in the grass when the Indian rides by.

You're a Poet? Then Show It!

Back in the distant past before television and the video cassette proved literacy to have only been a passing fancy, people wrote poems. Not poetry, exactly, not the epic stuff about the Forest Primeval or the Saga of Beowulf, but stories told or claimed, made in rhythm and rhyme.

Sometimes, as the poets or somebody said, their reach out-did their grasp, but that wasn't the point. The homespun poets had feelings and enthusiasm, and poems were how they expressed themselves. The author, who's committed a few limericks but no worse than that, used to work for a magazine whose editor finally ran an all-caps notice: NO MORE POEMS. PERIOD. What drove him to that extreme? Work like this:

INDIANS

There's many kinds of Indians (sic)
In this great and glorious land:
And many who are fleet of foot
Are found in every band.
They're noted for excessive speed,
For endurance and for strength.
Consider Thorpe of Olympic fame,
He set the pace for all.
And later a committee cast a vote
Which demonstrated heartless gall.
It seems to me the Indian
Is always on the run.
He's chased with locomotive,
Electricity and gun.
But now they've all been collared
Except one—and only one.
And all have given up the chase.
Because they're all outdone.
This Indian that I mention
Is an Indian known for speed.
From Atlantic to Pacific,
And is always in the lead.
There's nothing but the lightning's flash
Or the bullet from a gun
That ever yet approached the speed

If its ordinary run.
"To what tribe of Indian?" you ask,
Does this Indian now belong.
That has such speed and running powers
And is built so wondrous strong.
Tis the motocycle Indian
That leads in every race.
Tis the motocycle Indian
That always sets the pace.
and when you're talking Indian
Just remember this for fun,
That the motocycle Indian
Is the Indian that can run.

End of poem. It came from a copy made from a copy that was taken from a magazine or club bulletin or something like that, which is to say I haven't any idea who wrote it, sorry not to give credit where due.

There have been better poems written, in fact the other one, You'll Never Wear Out, is a better poem because it scans and can be easily memorized. But never mind that. What matters here is, that's how the fans felt about their brands then and how they let people know.

The Tourist Trophy and How It Grew

From its inception through to the end of our rivalry, the American Motorcyclist Association's Grand National Championship has been based on the Olympian principle that a real racer should be more than a specialist. The GN series has been based on points won on dirt ovals long and short, on road courses plain and fancy, and in events run on a closed circuit that include left and right turns plus at least one jump.

This event is called TT, which most racing fans know to be an abbreviation of Tourist Trophy. What's been lost in time is how rough-and-tumble dirt track racing got the name. Here's how:

Until the end of World War II, the United States was a motorcycle exporter and there was no balance of trade. Only a handful of imports, mostly from England, were sold here every year. One of the Britbike's leading exponents was a man named Reg-

Sport Scouts were often treated as raw material, to be modified as the owner wished. This one's owner has trimmed the rear fender, swapped the low Siamesed exhaust for two straight pipes, and added a luggage rack. Judging from the flag, the owner likes parades.

gie Pink. He was an importer, a dealer, and a stalwart of the Crotona, New York, MC. Pink had realized early on that the most important thing a motorcycle dealer can offer his customers is something to do with their motorcycles.

In England there was a form of horse racing, with turns and jumps, up hill and down, cross-country except it was a circuit instead of point to point, known as TT Steeplechase. In some measure because of this, when road racing for cars and motorcycles began on the Isle of Man just after the start of this century, the main event for motorcycles was called the TT, again short for Tourist Trophy and derived because the first races on the Isle of Man were up and down, cross-country, and on unpaved roads.

Pink and the other chaps knew all this. So in 1931, when times were hard and money short and professional racing out of the reach of the average rider, Pink and the Crotona MC borrowed an apple orchard near Somers, New York. They put on a race, through the orchard, up hill and down, airborne when speed and daring permitted. And because it reminded them of the Isle of Man and the horse racing that preceded it, they called the event a TT.

The sport of motorcycling was pretty much one family by 1931, largely because the sport was close to disappearing. Everybody knew everybody else. One of the riders invited to that first TT was a man named Ted Hodgdon, an enthusiast since his teen years, and in 1931 Indian's advertising manager. Hodgdon went to the TT, took notes and pictures and realized that everybody was having fun, while even better, all the riders had something to do with their motorcycles, the ones they'd ridden to the orchard.

Back in Springfield, Hodgdon told Indian's general manager Joe Hosley and sales manager Jim Wright all about it. Wright was also president of the AMA at the time; there were so few people in motorcycling then that if it hadn't been for conflict of interest, there wouldn't have been any interest. Hodgdon was also president of the Springfield MC, so he drew up a set of rules, sketched the course, reported the event, helped put on a TT with the Springfield MC, and published a story in the Indian News, while furnishing all the material to the AMA.

Next thing anybody knew, all the AMA clubs knew how to put on the new event, and when the production-based national rules appeared in 1934, TT was one of the classes. And we've raced TT ever since.

Racing Revives

Class C racing didn't merely create new interest in racing, it attracted a whole new bunch of riders, people who hadn't been in competition and probably wouldn't have been except it was so easy just to ride to the event and get on the bike. How new were they? One was named Ed Kretz. He rode his Chief to his first event, a TT, just like he was supposed to. He was doing good, too, until he crashed and broke the Chief's headlight. Next time, Kretz knew better. Before the start, he took off the headlight. So he crashed again and the bike landed on its saddlebag. Wanna guess where he'd packed the light? Right. And the next time we hear of Ed Kretz, he's winning the inaugural Daytona 200, in 1937.

In mechanical terms, the early tuners had lots to learn. Lubricating the V-twins was a challenge, in no small part because the pistons gallumping up and down inside the cylinders create tremendous pressure variations inside the crankcases, so the oil pump sometimes works into a vacuum, and sometimes contests a pressure of two atmospheres.

Early racers dealt with this the easy and crude way, by cutting holes in the cylinders below the pistons, venting the pressure into the atmosphere along with the oil. But the races were short and the riders got grimy anyway.

Early Sport Scouts (and other Indian twins) used a flapper valve, basic stuff. Harley-Davidson came out with a timed breather, by which the positive pressure could be used to push oil from the crankcase proper to the return side of the oil pump, as well as keeping internal pressure more-or-less constant.

When Class C racing began, the engines weren't ready for high speed and the cases used to fill with oil at full revs. Early tuners set the engines to under-deliver oil at speed, so the riders had to roll off and oil things down. The dirt tracks were ovals — converted, borrowed, or shared horse tracks—and the races were punctuated sprints, wide open on the straights, coast and oil through the turns.

Tuner Tom Sifton realized this needn't be. He solved the return and pressure problem with the timed breather, then instructed rider Sam Arena to keep the power on all the time. In 1938 Arena trimmed the record for the 200-mile Pacific Coast Championship, run on a mile track in Oakland, California, by 19 minutes, 20 seconds, which is about ten times the margin anybody's set a national record by, before or since.

This isn't to make fun of the other guys. There's never been an official measurement but experience says any advantage invented or discovered by any one tuner will become common knowledge within, on average, two races. The other guys looked and listened. Arena won lots of races after that, and Sifton became the best known and most successful tuner but he got out-run on a regular basis, just like the others.

The first point of this was that the sport increased. The owners had something to do with

their machines so they went to the races and rode in the races, some of them, anyway. It sounds impossible now but there were classes for 45s and for open bikes, the 61s, 74s, and 80s, in the TTs and hill climbs, and guys actually did it: they rode the 500 pound motorcycles, rigid rear wheels and handshifts, through the woods and across the deserts.

The serious guys went beyond that. Armando Magri, for one, finished work at the agency in California, rode his 61 to Illinois, rebuilding it along the way as needed, stripped the road gear off, raced and won, put the gear back on, rode home and reported to work on Monday (his boss was a racing nut so he pretended not to notice when Magri seemed tired).

The second point is that the bikes got better. Customers racing the product became a test fleet beyond imagination. And add to that the fact that when the buyer blew the thing up racing, he didn't blame the dealer or the factory, although he could

*S*port Scouts quickly came to fill the gap left by the disappearance of the 101 Scout, and they were the sports bike of choice until production ended at the beginning of World War II.

*L*egend-to-be Ed Kretz, just after winning the first Daytona 200 run in 1937, partially on the hard packed sand and partially on a poorly paved road parallel to the beach. His Sport Scout is in road-race trim, with brakes, a rear stand, and even a pouch for tools and parts: the pits could be a mile from a breakdown. *Hap Alzina Archives*

*K*ind of a last gasp for the board tracks. Leading here is Len Andres, whose family had a chain of H-D dealerships. He's riding a Harley RLD at the San Jose (California) Velodrome in 1937. The other chaps, also Harley mounted, have installed case guards. *Len and Brad Andres*

have, to some degree. When Indian began their in-house racing program, they put one of the then-new Sport Scouts on the engine stand, and opened it up. It lasted minutes, then BANG!

By the time they had special engines in production, the engines were tested before delivery and each one would hold up, without faltering or overheating, wide open throttle for half an hour, or it didn't get delivered.

Figures are deceiving here, especially since they can't be verified, but when Class C got underway, a WLD Harley seems to have been good for 30 horsepower, with less than 400 pounds to push, with even less bulk when you take off the lights and brakes and mufflers and so forth and no, it didn't take long for riders to leave their road gear in the pits. And by the time the tuners had done their work? Sifton always managed to beat the 37 horsepower of the factory's WLDR, which was the road model plus racing gear like magneto ignition and aluminum heads, and the race-ready bikes weighed not much more than 300 pounds.

Real Factory Racers

In 1938, the AMA declared Class C to be where the national championships would be awarded. Class A was the original factory pro class, originally raced on all of the tracks. By 1938, it was used only in speedway, by then run only on short tracks, with alcohol-burning singles.

Riders were no longer expected to ride to the track, race, and ride home, and most of the 45s used on the miles and half miles were stripped when new and left that way. The rules still required the parts to begin as production pieces and there came into being long lists of optional tanks and sprockets and cams and gears, all of which had to be cataloged and available for public sale. The speed parts were available, but only if the buyer knew what to ask for and found a dealer sympathetic to the cause.

There's an odd echo of the past here. Indian management decided to get into the racing business firsthand, with a run of special machines made for racing only. They began with a handful of bikes, which went direct to favored riders. The engine cases were different, with more volume in the crankcase—the art

ollister, California, later became famous for that biker-gang movie, but in the 1930s it was best known for motorcycle racing. This is 1937 and Len Andres, far left, is collecting the trophy he won earlier, which is why he's on his road bike and the other two riders, Al Torres and Jerry McKay, are on their TT 61s. The California Highway Patrol backed and endorsed racing then, which is why Officer Jack Cotrell is presenting the trophy. At far right is Dudley Perkins, pioneer H-D dealer in San Francisco. *Len and Brad Andres*

of controlling oil and air pressures inside racing V-twins didn't become a science for another 50 years—and the engines were known as Big Base Scouts.

This was, sorry to say, against the rules. It was a strange move, in that the production Scouts were lighter and more powerful than the Harley 45s. They won more races, albeit not always the major ones. And, as if to prove there is justice some of the time, these illegal Scouts appeared for Daytona 1941, and none of them finished the race, which, speaking of things to come, was won by a Norton.

The Milwaukee guys knew about the Big Base Scout, and there was some talk in the boardroom about H-D doing a short production run of race bikes. To Harley's credit, they did a more public extreme. In 1940, the hot model was the WLDR, W, L and D meaning the tuned engine in sport trim, the R meaning race stuff like alloy heads. In 1941, the hot model was the WR, W for the series, R for full race. Plus, there was the WRTT: flat track rules didn't allow brakes (or shifting gears, once the field was up to speed) while TT and road racing required brakes, as well as more miles per race.

The WR engine was full race, with special bearings, hot cams, high compression, and a host of speed tricks. The valves, for example, were canted toward the bore for less restriction on the flow. The catalog listed a bunch of special parts, like large and small oil and gas tanks and extra gears. In time there even came to be different frames.

Both factories have to have spent more on these separate-but-complimentary racing programs than they can have recouped in sales, never mind that by

this time the market had improved to the point where there were some modest profits. Not only that but the spirit of the Class C rules was being, um, stretched, in that in both camps, what had begun as racing production bikes was by 1940 producing racing bikes. And neither filed protests or blew whistles or pointed fingers at the other, maybe because they were both guilty and maybe (one would like to think) they enjoyed the sport of competition.

There was some subtle feuding in the ads, and in the house organs. Harley-Davidson, for instance, listed the Harley riders who finished, but the competition got blank space, no matter whether the rival was an Indian or one of the newly arrived English brands.

Indian was more clever, in that sometimes the INDIAN got all caps and Norton or Harley-Davidson got initial caps. Or, they'd all be listed except the only races reported were those won by Indian. But the best trick has to have been when *Indian News* not only reported Indians first through sixth, but gave the names of the Harley guys who trailed in seventh and eighth, plus the paper identified the two H-D riders whose mounts failed under the pressure.

*E*d Kretz and his Chief, at a TT, looking calm and fully in control (perhaps because he's removed his headlight *and* the saddlebags). Jerry Greer

$\mathcal{A}$ post-race contest. Armando Magri, left, and Jack Cotrell both have a hand on the winner's trophy at Oakland, California, 1939, because both guys think they were first over the line. The chap between them, looking as if he wishes he was someplace else, is Magri's indulgent boss, Frank Murray, from whom Magri will later buy the H-D agency whose jersey he has on here. Oh yeah, he took home the trophy. *Armando Magri*

$\mathcal{H}$arley-Davidson's WR, as plain and straightforward as its designation. The WR frame looks just like the WL version except the racing unit is made of thin-wall, better grade steel tubing. The WR as delivered weighed 100 pounds less than the WLD. The pad on the trimmed rear fender is so the rider can slide back and crouch on the straight. The huge magneto was made specially for Harley-Davidson and for this application. *Roy Kidney/Vintage Museum*

Chapter Thirteen

The Knucklehead and the "Improved" Four

Harley Captures the Flag

Before he became the creative power behind *Road & Track*, John R. Bond was an engineer at Harley-Davidson. He remained loyal to The Motor Company and in later years fondly recalled how many new and different motorcycles had been built inside the walls at Juneau Avenue, and how few of them had come out of the gates.

Reference has been made, for instance, to the notion of a four. A few years after that, one of the race-ready overhead valve 45s was tested in street form, complete with prop stands and toolbox, and—coincidence? I think not—while Harley's reps were helping Indian and the AMA plan Class C racing, the class with the sidevalve 750s and overhead valve 500s, H-D was testing an overhead valve conversion for the sidevalve 500 then being produced.

What made history, though, was that in 1931, when things were bad and getting worse, the founders, also known as the board of directors, made the best move they'd made since they got interested in motorcycles. They authorized work on a new and different and modern V-twin.

At about the same time, Indian made two major missteps, a short-term fumble in which they did something, and a long-term miscalculation, in which they *didn't* do something. In consequence,

Harley-Davidson took the lead in sales and earned a reputation for innovation.

H-D's good move began with the intent to strengthen the product line. They had the little single, doing well in the export market until protectionists overseas found out about it, the new and popular sidevalve 74s, and the not-quite-equal 45s. The founders decided to begin work on a 61, the traditional size from the J-series days. It would be overhead valve, and would have recirculating oil: when they warned against Indian's new system, they knew better, deep down.

The 61 was a national and world size and had been since MacAdam invented putting tar on roads. Overhead valves were more efficient and would allow higher compression ratios to take advantage of high-test gas. A 61 could be lighter and more agile than a 74, faster and less stressed than a 45.

The New Big Twin

The new engine was as modern as it could have been. Bore and stroke were 3 5/16x3 1/2 inches, nearly square, as they say. Earlier engines had longer strokes and smaller bores, in part because tradition says a long stroke gives more low-end grunt (it doesn't, not always).

*P*erhaps people simply didn't want four cylinders? The folklore reason for the sales failure of the upside-down Indian of 1936 was that the high and shielded exhaust and the tucked-beneath carb were ugly. *Jeff Hackett*

Up close and personal, it's easy to see why Harley's new overhead valve twin was named Knucklehead. The engine was separate from the gearbox, and it's not difficult to sight down the center of the row of pushrods and imagine the four-lobe, single-stick camshaft at the convergence of the vee. The chromed dome to the right of the pushrods is the ignition timer. © *Harley-Davidson Motor Company*

The valves were set at right angles to each other so they could be extra large, and to form a half-dome combustion chamber above the piston. The idea, known as a hemispherical combustion chamber, came from aircraft, and it's interesting now to look at a 1930s airplane engine and see how like the Harley design it was.

Of course the design, named the Model E because it followed the D series 45s off the drawing boards, was normal Harley, with air cooling, 45-degree vee, fore and aft cylinders on fork, and blade connecting rods sharing a crankpin. Have I mentioned that Harleys don't have crankshafts? They don't, not in the book. Harleys have pairs of flywheels. And they have timers, not distributors.

The engine was separate from the four-speed gearbox, with the two joined by a chain primary drive, tensioned by sliding the gearbox back and forth. And while we're being strict in terms, the new transmission had the gears fixed in place and the selection done by moving engagement dogs, so shifting gears was no longer being done. The frame was new, although it was drawn up from the first with the idea it could be shared with the sidevalve engines

The Model E was Harley-Davidson at its best and most bold, with a new frame and a new engine at the same time, along with the very latest in paint and design. Despite a few hitches, the Knucklehead was an instant sales hit. *Roy Kidney/Vintage Museum*

in time. There was more steel and welding, less cast-iron and brazing. The rear wheel was still fixed in place, while the forks, still leading link, had tubular legs instead of the older I-beam design.

Mechanical details are all very well, for example, the new engine had one camshaft with four lobes for less gear slop and noise, but the punchline here has to have been the styling. The Model E was right, from the start. The vee in the frame was packed with muscular engine, the trim tanks were enhanced by the instrument nacelle, the frame and exhaust pipes formed complementary speed lines, there was a generous choice of paint schemes, in two tone and with trim packages.

The Model E, and the EL with higher compression ratio, weighed a few pounds more than 500, with a wheelbase of 59 1/2 inches and a stylishly low seat height of 26 inches. Factory tests rated the E engine at 37 horsepower, the EL at 40, and claimed a stock EL would hit 95 miles per hour.

The E's rocker covers featured large nuts to hold the rocker shafts, again a feature seen on aircraft engines of the period. As soon as the faithful saw the engine, which was delayed a model year and thus was the object of much speculation, they decided the nuts looked like the business side of a clenched fist and called it the Knucklehead, a nickname instantly and permanently popular.

The Knucklehead was an immediate hit. It appeared in 1936, just as sales began to revive. There were the usual number of minor glitches and revisions, so many that they can't be detailed here. But that didn't matter.

The factory had to speed up the production line for the 61, which they were able to do, while the other models were also in short supply, This came as a surprise. If they ever read the notes of their meetings, the ones where the founders wondered time and again if they could justify the money spent on the 61, and the day they voted to keep going mostly because they couldn't afford not to, they must have thanked their lucky stars.

Indian Takes Two Strikes

One of the former Indian dealers interviewed for this book—who won't be named here because he's not as dumb as this makes him sound, was asked about Paul du Pont.

"Stripped the company and took off. You know how those rich guys are."

It would take the rest of today to come up with anything less fair than that. In actual fact, at about the time Harley-Davidson was tightening belts and drawing the 61, du Pont put up his own money—not the company's, not the stock, but his own cash—to help meet the payroll. Things were that tough. I mention this here because it's hard to understand how the Indian guys, who knew engineering and the market, could have gone so far off on this occasion.

The short-term bobble (and the second fumble, less directly) involved the Indian Four. There must have been lots of faith in the project. The Indian Ace was quickly updated and inducted into the family with Indian's own frame and front suspension. But the Ace/Henderson-designed engine remained. The Indian designers didn't like that. They had a better idea.

For 1936, the Four got a new engine. It still had one set of valves above and one set below, but they'd been turned upside down. The intake ports ran through the cylinders, up the side, and into the combustion chambers. The exhaust valves were in the head. This made engineering sense, in that the hot exhaust wasn't fed into the engine's metal but went direct to the airstream. The intake

benefited from the heat, as warmed fuel vaporizes better than cold fuel.

But the new engine looked odd. It was ugly, even, with extra shielding required to keep the newly freed heat off the rider, and with the carburetor sort of hanging off the lower half of the engine.

Legend has it that Indians have always had a good side, a photogenic side, on the right, with the less-appealing parts on the left, which is supposed to be why the factory always photographed the right side for the ads. The 1936 and 1937 Fours looked funny on both sides. Left side photos are rare, for whatever reason, thus their inclusion in this book.

For the next 50 years or so, history says that Indian was wrong because the engine looked odd and people didn't buy the new Four, which lasted only two years in upside-down form. But while the record shows not many people bought the upside-down Four in 1936 and 1937, the same record shows the Four didn't sell all that well in 1935,or 1939, or any model year. Police departments liked the Fours and bought them when they could, and so did some private parties with sidecars, but they never sold all that well. The time was wrong, and just

The Model E's frame is packed with engine. The tank for the now-circulating oil is below the seat in front of the rear fender, and the rectangular box behind the tank is the tool box. Roy Kidney/Vintage Museum

*H*and shifting is done carefully, by moving the shift lever to exactly where the proper position is marked and holding it there until the rider can feel that he has made the new selection.

*I*ndian's final Four, made in 1941, made good use of the ornate body panels shared with the Chief and Scout, ditto for the sprung rear hub. Note the massive oil sump at the bottom of the engine. There was no official word, but when the war ended, the Four disappeared. *Bob Stark*

because Honda turned the world upside-down with its Four in 1969 doesn't mean anything, same way the success of the VW Beetle in 1957 doesn't prove that Bantam shouldn't have failed to sell small cars to Americans in 1939. If people don't want to go to the movies, Sam Goldwyn is famously supposed to have said, you can't stop them.

The Real Mistake

Fifty years later, historian Jerry Hatfield thought the matter through. What if, he asked, Indian hadn't spent precious time and money on the Four? What if Indian had played not to weakness but to strength? What if Indian had done what Harley-Davidson did and invested in a new and improved big twin? The Chief was the class act at the time, selling well, and appreciated by those who couldn't afford one. What if Indian had gone modern in a manner people would have noticed?

This matters as much in perception as it does in fact. When the Model E was proving to have a strong engine, H-D got the notion of using it for record runs. The new racing rules were sort of hard

on the 61, and in fact about this time the fully-developed two-cam J engines were doing better, which led, in another of those coincidence-I-think-not items, to the banning of older engines, read here JH. The AMA said it was for safety reasons. Right.

But that's another chapter. Somebody in Milwaukee noticed that the official American speed record was 132 miles per hour, set in 1926 by Johnny Seymour on a four-valve Indian 61. Streamlining had been invented, and the Model E could easily be persuaded, with a second carb, hotter camshaft, and a magneto, mostly, to out-produce the old Indian. So Joe Petrali, the all-time winner, was assigned the job of taking the record from Indian.

Petrali and Hank Syvertson modified the engine and built bodywork; a disc for the front wheel, shields for the forks, and a tapering shell for the rear of the frame and the rear wheel. They went to Daytona Beach and the bike was clocked at 136.183 miles per hour, the fastest official normally aspirated motorcycle ever. The world's fastest motorcycle was still a supercharged BMW, but that didn't matter much to Harley and Indian. The run at Daytona took the American record away from Indian, which was all Harley-Davidson really wanted.

Closer to home, so to speak, Fred Ham rode a prepped, but production Model E 1,825 miles in 24 hours, averaging 76.02 miles per hour.

Harley-Davidson and Indian both had begun publishing house organs, official magazines, many years before this. Both were highly partisan. They

were much more interested in publicity than journalism. As could be predicted, Harley's magazine, *The Enthusiast*, was quick to trumpet the record runs, while being much slower to mention that the lovely bodywork, streamlining having just come into public vogue, hadn't worked and in fact had been removed for the actual record runs. The Knucklehead had done the job on power, and the frame and suspension could take what the engine dished out. The stock record, meanwhile, proved the new model's durability.

Indian Bites the Bullet

There was no official reaction from Springfield, but Hap Alzina, West Coast distributor, major dealer, the man who bailed out the company with a sackful of cash, and a man who believed in Indian, took matters into his own hands. He got one of the eight-valve 61s, devised a frame and suspension from various pieces of 101 Scout and board track racer. An aerodynamicist devised a complete enclosure, a shell that looked like a lima bean perched on edge.

This was a full streamliner, one of the first, and it went as far as the art/science then could take it. Rider Fred Ludlow had to set himself on the seat and the crew could then pop the two pieces of the fairing together, with the bike held upright by tiny retractable wheels. But the theory was better than the practice. With the tachometer indicating 145 miles per hour, the streamliner couldn't be controlled, and Ludlow had to roll off.

Alzina liked racing and Indians, but he was a family man and a conscientious man, not one who'd put an employee at risk, not even when taking the risk might teach Harley-Davidson a lesson. Alzina called Ludlow in, ended the attempts, and took the streamliner home, where it sat for years. (It's since been restored.) On the same trip, though, Ludlow set a record of 115.126 miles per hour on a Sport Scout and 120.747 miles per hour on a Chief, both Class C records. The machines had been carefully tuned by a top man, Red Fenwick (more about him later) and the bikes weren't stock. But because the cam and other changes were offered the next year, labeled Bon-

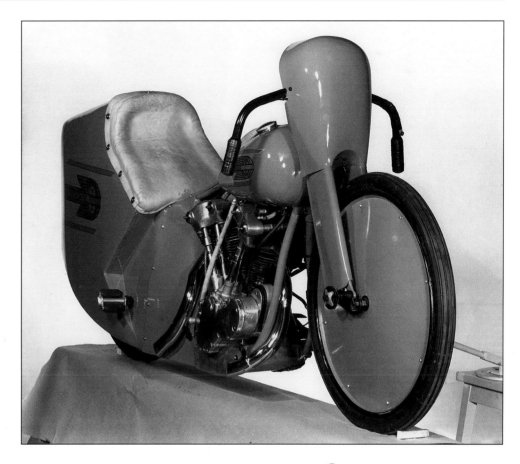

neville motors because that's where the runs were done, the machines could be called pre-stock.

Indian News made as much noise about these runs as the H-D organ had done about the Model E's record; well, *Indian News* used big letters for the Scout and Chief and sort of sloughed off the streamliner. But what mattered was Harley's records, the drama of Petrali crouched over the bars down the beach, of Ham riding 24 hours, round and round a five-mile circle, caught the public's attention. It was simply a fact that Harley's captive magazine had more readers than Indian's and a national record meant more than a class record.

The record proves the point. The 61 didn't just sell out that year and the next, it became the new flagship, the bike to have, and Harley-Davidson became the company from which the new stuff came. Over in Indian Country they referred to the Sixty-One as The Sickly One. But it didn't seem to help.

*S*treamlined Knucklehead was much more special than the factory liked to talk about, with a fully enclosed rear section, the windscreen, the wheel discs, the shields for the fork legs, the tiny damper for the fork links, the tuned straight pipes, and the magneto where the generator used to be. In the actual record runs, the body work was removed and the record was set by power and determination.
© *Harley-Davidson Motor Company*

Hap Alzina's non-factory streamliner was designed from logic outward: They built a mix of Scout and board-track racer, checked the profile, and built a shell to enclose machine and man. Tiny wheels kept it upright at rest and when getting under way, then they were retracted. (Later aerodynamic research indicated the design was too high and too short and later streamlined motorcycles would get the aerodynamics right and then somehow cram the man and machinery inside. Hap Alzina Archives

Photo from the day of the non-record shows the two halves of the shell and the ordinary sort of motorcycle that was inside the shell. The rider had to climb aboard and the crew then popped the two pieces together, and off he went. (The odd structure sticking up above the rear wheel is the front of the Indian Chief that ran for class records on the same occasion.) Hap Alzina Archives

$\mathcal{L}$ines and styling of the Model E were simply right from the start (this is a 1937 example). Paint and emblems reflected the Art Deco school, which was in vogue at the time. *Jeff Hackett*

$\mathcal{S}$tylish air horn kept out the larger debris. And yes, one did have to lift one's foot before applying the rear brake. *Jeff Hackett*

Chapter Fourteen

The Buddy Seat and the Chum-Me Seat

Little Differences and Ill Will

Back when the motorcycle was being collectively invented, for reasons now lost in time assuming there were ever any reasons, Indian put the throttle on the left and the gearshift on the right, while Harley-Davidson had the throttle on the right and the gearshift on the left.

In 1935 there was a Harley-Davidson option of left-hand throttle, right-hand shift. In 1936 Indian offered left-hand shift, right-hand throttle. No joke. Nor had both discovered at about the same time that they'd been wrong and the other chaps right. Instead, they were competing for the same market: government agencies, mostly police departments, and a few enthusiasts with firmly fixed prejudices, and both firms could see the benefit of not fighting to the death.

The earliest example of this is probably Indian's Dispatch Tow vs. Harley's Servi-car. They were three-wheelers, a motorcycle front end and engine backed by a two-wheel axle topped by a cargo box. Legend says the idea came because somebody at Parkard mentioned the bother of having to send two guys and a car when a dealership picked up a car for servicing—yes, they used to do that. Ask your granddad—Harley-Davidson first with Indian close behind, came up with the towable motorcycle,

allowing the go-fer to work alone. The police noticed and adopted the vehicle for parking meter enforcement, and cities used them for errands.

H-D's arrived in 1932, Indian's the next year, too close to have been a copy, and neither side hassled the other over it. The swappable throttles were because, well, supposed Manny is the mayor, Moe is his brother-in-law and a motorcycle dealer, and Jack is the city's purchasing agent. Manny wants Moe to have the city's business, so he tells Jack to specify motorcycles with 1,200cc, foot clutch, and so forth *and* left-hand or right-hand throttle, depending on which brand Moe deals in.

Am I saying there were politics in politics back then? Yes. Also chicanery, double-dealing, and dirty work at the crossroads. There are pages and pages of accounts of how Harley stacked the deck here, Indian did the same there, and Excelsior euchred them both someplace else. But by the late 1930s or early 1940s, because they had pretty much the same products and were competing for the same markets, the rivals seem to have come to terms.

That's at the top. As another example, the original passenger seats were second seats, perched way out on the rear fender. Then Harley-Davidson had an attack of genius and devised the

Perhaps more of a contradiction, when Indian slipped its full-race Sport Scout into competition, the production Sport Scout got the body panels, becoming sort of a Chief Jr. again. Not the sport it used to be, this final Sport Scout, circa 1942, wasn't as heavy as it looks. Roy Kidney/Vintage Museum

Harley-Davidson's Servi-Car was a useful device and a good seller when sales were slow elsewhere. The device on the forks, by the way, is the tow bar, which clamps on the town car's bumper so one man can pick up and deliver. H-D made this model for nearly 40 years.

Indian's version was very like Harley's, simply because the idea, the motorcycle engine and front end with axle and box behind, was so logical. The buyer had a choice of cargo box size, and this one is the big one. And you could get the Chief engine, which this one has.

Buddy seat, the tractor-style seat extended so two people could share it: Best part was when one person was of the opposite sex and if you jazzed the throttle and rolled off, she was pressed against you . . . ah, youth.

This was a wonderful idea. Indian had to have it and before you could say, "Wanna go for a ride?" there was an Indian option, the Chum-me seat.

The du Pont family and Allan Carter recall that the Harley people did some grumbling, or rubbed it in, but that Indian was allowed to make its double seat without any formal complaint.

The Crocker Incident

The exception in this era of good feeling (did I mention that by the late 1930s both surviving makes were showing modest profits?) involved an entrepreneurial engineer named Albert Crocker. Crocker was a gifted mechanic and thinker and Indian enthusiast and dealer. He had a first-class machine shop and did projects like overhead valve conversions for the Scout, then fuel-burning singles for speedway. When that faded, he began building full motorcycles for the street.

The Crocker was a V-twin, 45 degrees included angle, 61ci, and it arrived at the same time Harley's Model E came out. The two were similar, except that the Crocker had 53 horsepower and the Model EL had 40, which meant that the Crocker was the fastest production machine on the market, despite 1) Harley holding the record and 2) Crocker's production run of the first version totaled 17.

Not what you'd call a threat. Except that for some reason the guys at Harley-Davidson didn't like the idea. Historian Harry Sucher says Joe Petrali told him H-D management arranged to borrow a Crocker and had Petrali dismantle it, watched by a lawyer and photographer, in case Crocker had used some Harley parts or patents. They found nothing of the sort.

Milwaukee's next step was to lean on the firm supplying wheels to Harley, Indian, and Crocker, telling them to choose between H-D and Crocker. Neither of these not-very-nice moves appear in the board's notes—which isn't surprising— but the business with the wheels is confirmed by the du Pont family and by Allan Carter.

He says yes, there was such a flap, but Paul du Pont thought it was both unfair and foolish to interfere with Crocker, and du Pont simply arranged to be the middleman for the wheels, so either Crocker or his customers could get them through Indian.

Walter Davidson blustered, Carter remembers, but bluster was all he did and the trading of parts and ideas continued.

There were other divergences, if not quite rivalries. The prewar economy had improved and there was a flurry of fashion, as in General Motors inventing the styling studio and building special large and flashy vehicles for show but not sale.

Indian's chief designer then was G. Briggs Weaver, an engineer who'd been with du Pont in the car company and transferred over. It had been a productive partnership. Weaver, according to Carter, was a daring visionary and du Pont had a good grasp of the practical.

Indian took back the lead in innovation, as the Four and the Chief got rear suspension, with the rear hub moving up and down on springs held by the rear of the frame. There wasn't a lot of motion, but it did absorb the worst blows the roads dealt out. Quoting from *Motorcyclist's* review: "The motorcycle with a rigidly mounted rear wheel cannot possibly offer the riding qualities of a machine with a sprung rear wheel, the other factors being equal. That is too elementary to require further elaboration."

Perhaps so. Too bad they weren't there to say that in 1913.

But the sprung hub was an idea whose brief time had come, as the English and Germans were doing the same thing.

Indian expanded on the paint still again, with glorious two-tone schemes, paint with metallic mix, and something called the "World's Fair Streamline" tank design. (The World's Fair was held in New York in 1939, and Indian was far from the only company to exploit the event.)

Most visible of Indian's changes was the styling. Again, this echoed what cars were doing, as the Four, the Chief, and even the Scout acquired lovely, swooping enveloping fenders, in the fashion of French coach builders. Even today, if there's one thing the average person can spot, it's the fully valanced, semienveloped, two-tone Indian Chief.

The Clubs Compete

Harley-Davidson meanwhile soldiered on, making small and useful improvements to the 45s, 61s, 74s, and 80s, which filled the middle of the

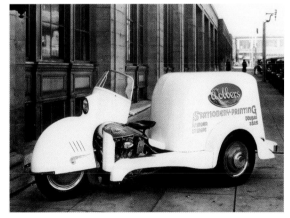

market and sold better than the smaller or larger rivals, domestic or imported.

There was another divergence, a new line that cut through the Indian-Harley division. The clubs, one make or regional, were very strong and active and there came to be sort of a split in that some groups were rowdies, unkempt, and liable to ride their bikes in pastures or across sidewalks. In a reaction to this, there came to be family or couple clubs, with emphasis on precision riding and on outfits, with mom and pop color-coded to match each other, their bike (of either make), and the other members of their club. Along with events like riding a plank or seeing who could ride the slowest and not put down a foot, there were contests for best-dressed couple and club.

You didn't have to settle for what the factory supplied. This motoricksha is a Dispatch Tow with the cargo box carved into dual seats complete with commodious floorboards. *Hap Alzina Archives*

Here someone has taken a trafficcar, the police version of the Dispatch Tow, and converted it into a delivery van with full, well nearly full, weather protection. A Chief with teepee, somebody wrote in the family album, but we wouldn't dare make a joke like that now. *Hap Alzina Archives*

The Crocker was a work of art. Clearly inspired by racing, the road model was the fastest motorcycle on sale in 1936, with more power and less weight than Harley's new 61. But Crocker couldn't make many, and few people could afford those he made, so the brand lasted only a few years and served only to inspire and to make Harley-Davidson angry. *Cycle World*

The Chief's sprung rear hub was a genuine mechanical advance, while the elaborate and fanciful paint and the sweeping body work made the big Indian instantly recognizable on the road, to the extent that this is what everybody thinks when they think Indian.

For historical purposes, note that after World War I, Howard Hughes made a movie about air combat titled *Hell's Angels*, and in 1938 a motorcycle club in Detroit adopted the name. The name seems to have been taken in the spirit of play, because in 1938 the Hell's Angels Motorcycle Club won the AMA award for safety, as in the most member miles ridden without injury or accident. The outlaws and dopers so beloved by Hollywood, and so useful to motorcycling's critics, were still to come.

Prosperity hadn't arrived yet either, which may be why the real rivalry during this time wasn't at the top but in the middle at the dealerships. This rivalry wasn't corporate policy. It can't have been, because it depended on who ran the place more than what sign on the building said.

Len Andres, whose family had Harley stores up and down California, says in the 1930s when he was the Harley-Davidson dealer in Modesto, his peer

This photo was taken during an outing from Hap Alzina's headquarters. It was a long and dusty ride but even so, these guys look like the guys you'd want on your side when push came to roundhouse right, eh? *Hap Alzina Archives*

Here comes the Harley-Davidson club, neatly attired in matching outfits for men and women, black boots for the guys and white for the gals. They are parading onto the track before the national race at Langhorne, Pennsylvania, in 1940, and they are on purpose as much of a contrast to the rowdies shown next door as they could possibly have been. © *Harley-Davidson Motor Company*

127

The W series Harley-Davidsons were mostly improved versions of the earlier 45s, with the major exception of the recirculating oil system introduced with the Model E. *Ron Hussey*

This example is a late model 1951 and has been fitted with every extra: windshield, buddy seat, crash bars, and so forth. H-D's thinking was the WL buyer would like a smaller version of the full-dress 74s, and a lot of buyers did. *Ron Hussey*

in Merced, which wasn't that far away, had strong feelings on the issue.

"He didn't like Indians or the guys who rode in on 'em. He used to tell them to get their oil-soaked wrecks out of his clean driveway. A lot of his customers came down and bought bikes from me."

Andres says it wasn't a Harley-Davidson deal.

"The guy who owned the Harley store in San Diego before I bought it went to meet the Indian dealer there. Thought they were in the same business, they ought to know each other. The Indian dealer told him to get back to his own store and stay there. It worked both ways."

Does this sound like foolishness? It sounded the same way even back then, to those who'd thought it out.

Len Andres again: "How are you going to get new people if you aren't polite to the people you haven't got yet?"

Chapter Fifteen

The 841 and the Model XA

Shot Down by Friendly Fire

Forget Pearl Harbor: Indian and Harley-Davidson were busy with the war effort even before anybody knew where Pearl Harbor was, never mind what she did.

Seriously though, most everybody with brains enough to pour rainwater from their boots could tell war was going to happen. And there were people in charge in the United States who did their best, against popular opinion, to get us ready.

Motorcycles had proved useful in World War I and the Army had a small fleet in the 1930s, so before any shots were fired, the military invited motorcycle makers to submit ideas for scout and/or combat two-wheelers.

By happy chance, du Pont and Weaver already had something on the drawing board. His family says du Pont was always interested in new ideas and he realized that a 90-degree V-twin, being in perfect primary balance, could make a good motorcycle engine. Indian's engineering department began drawing up such a design, in hopes of attracting money for development when presto, there came the army. There are no formal records of this, but it does sound in character.

Meanwhile, the American motorcycle companies knew what was going on elsewhere, although they didn't always have the money or the reasons to do what the other chaps were doing. This wasn't always bad, as we'll see any minute now.

The Bikes (Almost) of Tomorrow

Indian began its military prototype with the idea of the well-balanced twin, and came out with a model designated the 841: 8 for the new engine and 41 because that was the year it was supposed to be produced.

It was an sidevalve 750, with 90-degree included angle and with the crankshaft aligned fore and aft in the frame, so the cylinders were at a right angle in the chassis. Because the army had had trouble with drive chains earlier, the specs called for shaft drive, which is one reason the engine sat crossways in the frame.

Meanwhile, somebody in England had invented the positive-stop gearshift, which made foot shift practical, and clutches had been improved so the springs that held the engine's power could be controlled by a hand. The 841 therefore had foot shift and hand clutch, along with the sprung rear hub and a stout version of the Sport Scout's girder forks.

Harley-Davidson was, as usual, more conservative. The guys there knew the military had been impressed with the German BMW and with an American version of same, so the Harley-Davidson

The facts aren't as impressively fearsome as this training photograph appears. In the real war it proved impossible to ride a motorcycle and fire a submachine gun at the same time (look closely and you'll notice the tommy guns don't have magazines). The motorcycle did useful work in the war, running errands and delivering messages, perhaps some scouting here and there, but the motorcycling cavalry went no further than this. © Harley-Davidson Motor Company

While actual motorcycles were being ridden in training, the makers were also involved in projects. This tricycle was one of Indian's experiments, with Chief engine and gearbox and two rear wheels so the rig wouldn't fall over. And then came the Jeep, which ended the experiments. One odd gain, though, was that the military insisted that Indian reveal its technical details, which it had always kept locked up. So owners back then and restorers since have been able to learn what went where.

military prototype was an outright copy of the German machine.

Following the Harley-Davidson system, the military bike was the XA: X for the engine series, A for the army. (H-D has used X for engines three times in 93 years, D and F twice, H and a few other letters, never.)

The XA was a flat twin with opposed cylinders across the frame and was also a system in perfect primary balance. It was also sidevalve, with shaft drive, hand clutch, and footshift. The first versions used leading link forks but later ones had Harley's first telescopic front suspension, and all XAs had sprung hubs, like Indian's.

In terms of commercial rivalry, Indian fired the first shot or won the first battle when the French ordered 5,000 Indian Chiefs with sidecars. This took place well before the United States formally entered the war or even started to put our military might in gear.

Remember the mention of what the other guys were doing? During their depression, the French made only economy motorcycles, little tiddlers, so when their army needed big, strong pack-bikes, they had to import them. This was a tremen-

dous boost for Indian. It was a bigger order than they could handle at first, so they had to reactivate part of the plant. But they filled the order, shipped the bikes, and got the money. It was the best thing that happened during the war for both makes.

War is nothing if not urgent, so most of this history happened in parallel, that is, while Harley and Indian were building their prototypes, they were also making three-wheeled scout/errand vehicles and modifying conventional machines for military use.

Indian lost this one. For some reason Indian believed the United States wanted 500cc machines, so they submitted the Junior Scout, equipped for war. It proved overburdened for the job. Harley-Davidson meanwhile offered the 750 WL because William Harley predicted, correctly, that the 500 wouldn't be big enough so there was no sense wasting time and effort.

As it happened, Harley-Davidson got the American order, for the WLA for army and WLC as in Canada, while the English and other allied forces bought thousands of Indians, in 500cc form. That part, seeing as how both brands sold to the military at a time when the government had shut down civilian production, was a modest gain for both.

Then the first worst happened. While the army had been experimenting with motorcycles, the prototypes and the modified, they'd also been trying off-road four-wheelers. In short and compressed order, the army learned that motorcycles make lousy combat vehicles, and that the new project did everything motorcycles didn't. It was, of course, the Jeep.

The Jeep would go anywhere, carry anything, didn't tip over, and was so easy and simple to operate that even an officer could do it. There are those who said the Jeep won us the war. What the Jeep also did was send Indian and Harley home from the front lines. As soon as it was clear the motorcycle wasn't suited for combat and that the Jeep was a better pack mule, the War Department canceled the projects, settled for the modified production bikes, and even declared surplus some of the motorcycles already built.

Cavalry 2, Indian 0

In terms of our rivalry, World War II was a draw, in that both makes sold some motorcycles to the military, both got some engineering practice, and both lost money when the military projects were canceled. It's probably just as accurate to guess that Indian made a good profit in selling the 5,000 Chiefs with sidecars, because that was simply production with little design or investment required.

Even so, Indian lost the war. To see how, turn to *Indian News*. The house organ billed itself as the voice of 100,000 riders, that presumably being the number of Indian owners or fans who got or read the paper, which came out monthly until the war powers took the newsprint and slowed the Indian paper to every two months.

Most of the news was just what you'd expect, as in there were pictures from Indian owners at the front, or in camp. And the guys overseas or in camp got news from home; there was a feature article about a woman who rode her Indian to military bases, delivering cigarettes (imagine how that would go over 50 years later). And there was news of an Indian-powered toboggan, sort of a proto-snowmobile.

But *Indian News* was a house organ, frankly—well, most of the time—devoted to promoting Indian motorcycles. Thus, along about the time the 841 was being designed and presented to the army, *Indian News* has a technical article explaining why a 90-degree twin was better than, oh, let's say a flat twin. There was no mention of Harley's flat twin; instead

they took aim at the BMW and Zundapp (they were German, get it?).

Paul du Pont had an early version of the 841, done as a civilian machine, and he rode it around, visiting people and letting them look at the project. Most were impressed. When they weren't, to give the *Indian News* editor credit, the paper ran the letters. For instance, one hard-core took aim at the "panty-waists who are in favor of hand clutch, foot shift and other fol-de-rol... Indian is a good old American name and exclusively an American bike."

Luckily, the guys in charge pressed on. Quoting an ad in the paper, "Out of the experience being gained in this war is being born a new Indian, a machine with brute power, strength and built-in guts to stand up under the most terrible punishment of war, a motorcycle you will be proud to own when this war is finally won."

Then came the blow. Not only had the 841 not won the contest and the contract for full production, not only had the project been canceled, but the military or the government or somebody, whoever had set up

Indian's military proposal was underway before the war began. The 841 was a sound set of ideas and a radical departure from convention at the same time. Visible here are the cross-mounted 90-degree v-twin and shaft drive, along with the sprung rear hub and girder forks derived from the Chief and Scout. This example was Paul du Pont's own bike. Roy Query/the du Pont family

Harley-Davidson's military prototype was a straightforward copy of the German BMW opposed twin, which at the time was doing effective work in the African desert, especially when rigged with sidecar and powered third wheel. This early version has the sprung rear hub seen on no other H-D before or since and a stamped steel version of standard leading link forks. © Harley-Davidson Motor Company

*W*e saw it here first, so to speak. Just above the floorboard is the rocker shift, on the left. And the lever on the left grip is the clutch lever. And just in case (hint) there seems to be some space in the engine bay, DuPont had plans for the 841 frame. *Roy Query/the du Pont family*

E. Paul du Pont on his 841. Late in the war, after Indian had done its part and paid for it, du Pont rode the 841 around the country, visiting dealers and friends and showing them what he cheerfully hoped would be the future for Indian when peace returned. *The du Pont family*

the deal in the first place, pulled the plug. Not only would there be no orders, the cost of doing the work so far, of designing and building and testing, was Indian's cost. No more federal money, period, and oh yeah here's a prize and a banner for the guys at the plant.

This was tough. This was something Indian literally couldn't afford. There was nowhere near as much bother back in Milwaukee, where they'd also expected to win the contract

and been stuck with the costs of the work done, but *The Enthusiast* hadn't shown Walter or William riding XAs around town. Harley-Davidson had built the XA because they were asked to and there was a war on.

Indian the company bore up as well as Indian the stereotype stoic. The ads shifted. They urged readers to "Buy War Bonds now, to buy an Indian later." Chiefs and Scouts in 45 and 30-50 models are listed, and the ad says they "will be ready for you after the war is won."

But there's no mention of that all-conquering, new and improved motorcycle proclaimed so happily six months earlier.

Indian's basic military model was the 741, the 500cc version of the Scout engine. Indians were built in the thousands and were sent to U.S. allies in this form and as the 640B: same chassis and engine except with 45ci. This example is painted olive gloss, as the military specified for parade duty. *Cycle World*

The U.S. Army's actual workhorse motorcycle was the Harley WLA, basically the civilian 45 with raised suspension and a giant (and effective) oil bath air cleaner. *Cycle World*

Chapter Sixteen

The Hummer and the Indian CZ

Too Little, To Soon

Not to use the punch line as the opening remark, but if there's a moral to be drawn from this chapter, it's that being close isn't nearly as good in the motorcycle business as it is in horseshoes and hand grenades.

World War II officially ended the way it began, as in War-click-Peace. In real life it wasn't nearly that clear and clean. Indian and Harley-Davidson had been eased out of the war effort, not by bad intent but by circumstances. Even when they were doing war work, both firms had naturally been thinking about what would happen next.

The end of the war unleashed hopes and prospects of a magnitude unparalleled in human history. As one small part of the whole, motorcycling enjoyed a boom the like of which hadn't been seen since the motor captured the bicycle. Both American makes knew something like that was going to happen. How they acted and reacted to the arrival of peace and prosperity was partially similar, but mostly different.

Harley's good moves began with war reparations, by which the winners get to collect what they might find useful, for instance the 125cc two-stroke single being built by DKW, one of Germany's several motorcycle makers. Harley-Davidson in the United States (and BSA in England) was granted permission to use the design. The reason, for H-D and BSA, was

simplicity itself: If the kid can pay for it, he'll buy it. Entry level, as they came to say later.

Harley-Davidson took the design and built the machine, coded M-125 or S-125 and later named the Hummer, at home. It was basic, with seat for one and the very minimum of lights and such and it was, oh, three-quarters modern, in that it had hand clutch, foot shift, leading-link forks, and rigid rear wheel.

Harley-Davidson was operating in the traditional way, one small step at a time. There were plans on the boards and prototypes being tested, but for the immediate period—the 125 came out in 1947—H-D management realized there was no rush; all those guys fresh out of service with cash in pocket would buy what they could find. So the 125 was new, the big sidevalve twins were dropped from the lineup, the E and EL 61s were joined by 74-cubic-inch versions for the overhead valve engine, coded F and FL. There was the familiar W series and the WR for racing. This made sense, as Milwaukee's stodgy strategies so often seem to do.

Moving out of time and beyond our feud for a bit, the 125 did its job and sold well in the early going, only to fall victim to lack of interest on the collective part of the dealerships, who didn't like singles or the kids who came in to ride them. But that's another history.

Neither the words, "cool" nor "dude" were in common use back in the 1940s, but the concept, the "Cool Dude," had been invented. This is a Harley-Davidson press photo, produced to show the public that clean-cut kids could have fun on motorcycles. The bike was dubbed the Hummer, and was initially available with a 125cc engine (shown above). A 165cc version was released later. © *Harley-Davidson Motor Company*

Only a handful of Indian's proposed postwar X44 engines were made before the company changed hands and the design was abandoned. That seems beyond mere regret, as the engine looks right, even now. It was 61ci, overhead valve, with the intakes inside the corral of rocker boxes, and one carburetor atop the center. There were two exhaust ports, one per cylinder on each side, so there are two exhaust manifolds to feed a pair of mufflers. *Roy Query/the du Pont family*

The X44 had the crankshaft surrounded by the crankcase; it had to slipped inside from one end. Then the cylinders were bolted on to the assembly. The X44 used magneto ignition, visible here, and was air cooled, witness the generous finning. The X44 engine was installed in at least one 841 frame for testing. *Roy Query/the du Pont family*

Indian Plans Big

Indian's plans were more complicated, something we see again and again in this 50-year contest. The same circumstances, literally millions of people with money and time for the first time in years. And Indian's most basic move was uncannily like Harley's, in that Indian bought the rights to a 125cc two-stroke single. It was made by CZ, the Czechoslova-

kian firm, and it had four speeds forward, footshift, hand clutch, plunger rear hub, and telescopic forks.

It was known as the Indian CZ, pronounced "check" because Cee-Zee or Cee-Zed were too European. And, like the Hummer, it wasn't what Indian dealers had in mind. What Indian's management had in mind was much larger than that.

Weaver, who'd been the head engineer since the ill-fated upside-down four, was a daring and creative man. He and du Pont shared enthusiasm for new stuff, although du Pont was, as will be unhappily evident, more practical. During the war, with the time not needed to refine or produce the 841, Indian's design department had been working on a whole new engine family, with a four, a twin, and a single.

The actual 841 wasn't part of the plan. The official recall, so to speak, from insiders like Allan Carter and from former dealers and fans, is that the 841 engine would have been too expensive, what with having to pay for tooling and tool-making, and an 841 would have to have sold for several hundred dollars more than the competing FL Harley, which had already been paid for.

The du Pont and Weaver plan was to use the 841 frame powered by an entirely new four, with that engine's dimensions and internals repeated: the 61-cubic-inch four, a 30-50 twin, and a 15-cubic-inch single. The plan was well underway, witness the test engine shown nearby, when in 1945, everything came to a stop.

Paul du Pont Departs

This is another one of those financial deals, tremendously complicated and too intricate to explain here. (That means the author isn't sure he understands it.) But another industrialist, Ralph B. Rogers, had gained control of what was still officially the Indian Motocycle Company. The timing was off, in that when the buy was actually made, some of the du Ponts were out of the country, and the notes from the period leave an impression of a hostile takeover.

Carter and the next generations of du Ponts say this isn't exactly true. Paul du Pont had owned

The du Pont family's 841s did all sorts of duty, including, to judge from the license plate bolted to the fender and the number on the forks, the occasional enduro. That's son Lex, who must be getting ready to ask dad if he can borrow the bike. The du Pont family

Indian for 15 years, and during that time the company had 1) remained alive and 2) lost an aggregate $260,000. Joe Hosley, who'd run Indian for du Pont, had died, and du Pont didn't feel any obligation to others in the firm. There's an impression that the old-timers, whose jobs du Pont had saved, never forgave him for it.

The younger du Ponts liked motorcycles but that's not the same as wishing to own a company that makes them, so while son Lex owns bikes and takes care of family heirlooms like the Indians shown here, his business is aviation.

In any event, Paul du Pont may simply have been tired. He wasn't in good health by 1945 and died five years later. By any and all accounts, he'd done more for Indian than has been generally appreciated, and he surely did more for Indian than Indian did for him.

The Belt Gets Tightened

Rogers, the new owner, was an astute businessman, an experienced executive and industrialist, and like du Pont, a motorcycle enthusiast. But he doesn't seem to have known much about motorcycles or the markets they sell in. In still another echo of the past, Rogers owned or controlled various manufacturing companies that made diesel engines, air conditioning units, lawn mowers, and so on. He was at home with industrialism and moved Indian to a better and more efficient (or so they hoped it would be) factory.

What Rogers didn't do was make motorcycles. The CZ contract expired and wasn't renewed. There were no more Dispatch Tows. Production of the fours had stopped when the war began and never resumed.

Surely worst of all was that the Scout—remember the promises in the ads?—didn't go back into production. The dealers asked, then demanded, and

Harry Sucher says they invaded the board meetings, so much did they believe in the Sport Scout. Indian's owners had to call the cops to keep out the dealers. But the board held firm, no more Scouts.

Instead, when Indian resumed motorcycle production, it was only the Chief. There were some modest changes, mostly a version of the 841's front suspension, girder forks on the lines of the Sport Scout's, which in turn began way back with the Prince. Even so, the accounts of the day say it made the Chief handle more predictably.

And the poor dealers sold all the Chiefs they could get for whatever consolation that was.

E. Paul du Pont, late in his life. Paul du Pont held several patents and manufactured marine engines, cars, and motorcycles during his career, and when he gave instructions in how to make things, he knew of what he spoke. *The du Pont family*

*T*he rules allowed hillclimbers to be pretty much what the builder wanted. This is a Knucklehead 61, in a stretched frame and with later-model telescopic forks. There's just the one gear in the box, and the rider clunks it into gear, stomps the clutch pedal, and hits the hill wide open.

*A*n Indian Scout formed the basis for this hillclimber, but the factory provided the special frame and front suspension, as used on factory racing machines. The magneto ignition is mounted high and out of harm's way, where the generator used to be. *Roy Kidney/Vintage Museum*

Chapter Seventeen

Racing, Part II

The Speedy Scout Versus the Long-Lived WR

Minutes before the big race at Spencer, Iowa, in 1947, Harley racer Leo Anthony took the gearcase cover off his WR and all the cams fell out. Nobody knew what to do because the book said to replace the cams you had to get the valves out, and that meant taking the cylinders off the sidevalve engine and there wasn't enough time.

Indian racer Bill Tuman stepped into the breach and began putting the cams back into place.

"You can't do that, " the Harley crowd said.

"Do it all the time," Tuman said.

The last nut went home, they rode to the line, and just as Hollywood wouldn't dare have happen, Leo Anthony won for Harley, with Tuman second for Indian. And that, as the sort of story that has to be true proves, is how it was then. Great stuff, in other words.

Motorcycle racing in the 1940s and 1950s was kind of like stock car racing in the 1980s and 1990s, in that first, everybody played fair by the real-if-unwritten rules; second, the original rules and format weren't even glanced at; and third, all the fans pretended not to know that what they were watching wasn't what they pretended it was.

By the end of the war both Indian and Harley-Davidson (as well as the imports, rapidly becoming a factor) had pretty much decided that there was no longer any point in having the racers buy road machines, strip them, and ride to the races.

Indian formalized this with the Big-Base Scout, first handed out in semisecret and in 1948 formalized by a production run with 50 examples, officially designated 648. Of course the machines were parceled out to selected riders; that is, the public didn't actually have a look in, but on the other hand there weren't more than 50 riders, if that many, who had the ability to use the machine.

And Harley-Davidson had the WR, sold stripped and ready, and with a tremendously long list of special parts and equipment. They were legal, except in this case, most people didn't know what to ask for, nor did dealers have the racing parts in stock. But that didn't matter. This new and improved golden age of racing was a four-part pyramid:

At the top, in the councils of the AMA and the factories, was fair play. Racing was run, OK ruled, by the AMA's competition committee, comprised of men from the factories, importers, dealer, riders, promoters, and suppliers.

Len Andres, who was on the committee as a dealer and tuner, sat at the table with Walter Davidson. Not once, Andres recalls, did Davidson ever

Typical slam-bang action as Floyd Emde, 7x, throws the rear wheel of his brakeless Harley-Davidson WR so far to the outside that he gets away from his left foot, which has a steel plate on its boot and should be acting as a guide or a pivot, the way #24 is doing up close to the rail. This is 1947, Reading, Pennsylvania, and it's typical of the track and the hard-fought competition of the period. Don Emde

*T*his the photo was submitted to the AMA by Indian to establish exactly what the 648 Scout looked like. It has the brakes, a rear stand, full fenders, and large oil and gas tanks so it can be used for road races. Most of that will be taken off for the flat track events. Every piece, though, had to be documented. *Don Emde*

*O*ne (the only?) benefit to not having rear suspension was that the machine could be really low to the ground, witness this Sport Scout, stripped for flat track. *Jeff Hackett*

suggest to him how he should vote, nor did Davidson remind Andres of certain shared interests.

In fact, the time Andres remembers best was when Davidson moved to change short track to 250cc singles, and the other members reminded him that Harley-Davidson didn't make a 250.

The 750s were too big, Davidson grumbled, and too many boys were being hurt. His motion carried and if H-D later made a 250 that was a winning short track mount, well, it shows that sometimes if you take care of the chicken, you get better eggs.

This atmosphere of sporting tolerance led to the unwritten rules, and neither side fussed over what the other did, as long as there was good reason for it. The unwritten rule was simple: blatant low-tech cheating was out and would earn the scorn of those the riders and tuners hoped would be peers and friends. But if it was clever, it was overlooked.

One example was the Scout/Chief relationship. The Harley engines, the overhead valve 61 and sidevalve 74s, 80s, and 45s, were very different engines, related only in basic stuff. But the Scout and Chief were big and little brothers. It wasn't that tough to put a 74-cubic-inch Chief engine in a Sport Scout frame. It was even easier to use Chief flywheels in Scout cases. The engine looked stock but the 45-cubic-inch engine had grown to 57 and such a bike would outrun the Chief as well as a stock Scout.

This was done on the street and in street racing and for some forms of competition where displacement was the only rule. Where it wasn't done was Class C, where 57 cubic inches would have been nearly unbeatable.

Why didn't anybody do it? First, to hear it from those who were there, it would have been obvious. The riders and tuners knew their stuff and the exhaust note would have been instant exposure. More to the point, it was too easy. What mattered was being clever, resiting the engine in the frame for better balance, making stiffer mounting plates to get rid of flex, and building your own frames that looked like the factory's but had the engine where you wanted it.

Meanwhile, the actual rules allowed cam grinding, port reshaping, combustion chamber contouring, and so on, while at the same time, careful and skilled balancing and assembly was probably the best secret.

In general, the Scout was lighter and faster and the WR was stronger and more durable. The Harley guys took stuff off and shaved down what they couldn't throw away, and the Indian guys used Harley parts.

Yes, part of this was copying. The WR engine used four one-lobe camshafts, one beneath each valve. The Scout had two camshafts, sited between the pairs of valves and with one lobe working rockers, one side for intake, the other for exhaust.

The clever guys made the single lobes on the Indians into two lobes, each half as wide, which gave

*I*nteresting contrast, the dirt track Sport Scout shown here versus the all-options-fitted example on the previous page. *Jeff Hackett*

each valve the individual timing needed. The Big-Base Scouts had different (and lighter and stronger) flywheels from the stock Scout, but the racers swapped the Scout's roller bearings for ball bearings, WR style. And the fastest Indians used Harley-Davidson crankpins and other lower-end parts. It was no secret. Sure, they'd say, it felt odd at first having Harley parts in my Indian, but then I noticed the engine didn't blow up any more and it no longer seemed so strange.

Not only did Harley-Davidson not mind, they didn't rub it in.

The Talent Pool

One reason for the sporting forbearance was that the pro racers, the second level of the four, all tell the same story.

They were attracted to motorcycles. A dad, a big brother, a neighbor, had a motorcycle and let them ride and they liked it. Because the Class C rules opened competition to all comers, they could try it out at small cost or risk. Carroll Resweber, who'd go on to win the national title four times, rode his stroked UL to the races, got showered with dirt, and decided that's what he wanted to do. Bobby Hill, who won 11 nationals and took home the Number One

Some different things were a lot alike. These three Indian teamsters are, from left: Ed Kretz Jr., Jimmy Kelly, and Ted Evans, all aboard 648 Indians at Southern Ascot Speedway, South Gate, California (there were at least three tracks in southern California with the Ascot name in them). Hap Alzina Archives

And here are three Milwaukee stalwarts at Milwaukee's mile track, since paved, alas, in 1947. John Butterfield, Billy Huber, and Pete Chann are on WR Harleys, and they have that cheerful confidence so evident in the Indian camp. Perhaps one reason we have races is to know who is fast, and who just looks fast. © Harley-Davidson Motor Company

plate twice, began riding Harleys in a motorcycle club. He rode club events for two years, then won his first seven races, but couldn't find a Harley to ride after the war. An Indian dealer offered him a Scout, and away he went.

Professionalism is relative. Few of the riders on either side made real money, not like the stars after full-time sponsorship arrived, but it was better than the farm. Ed Kretz had a subsidy from Indian, when Indian could afford him. Harley-Davidson had a racing department to hand out parts and advice to those who'd earned approval, but for the most part the riders were supported by themselves, the tuners, and the dealers.

The championship circuit was a traveling circus and the guys swapped parts, loaned each other money, and took each other to the hospital or home when required.

"It was fun, " Bill Tuman says. "It was tooth and nail on the track, beer and jokes after the races."

Still Rivals

Even though the brand name was less important than the real struggle, which was between the riders and the referees and promoters, there was some entertainment value in Us vs. Them.

Erwin Smith, known as Smitty when he was a dealer and tuner of Indians in the 1940s, says "I never saw anybody on either side try to hurt anybody, or make anybody get hurt. But they would try to beat you."

And they'd use psychology, as if when someone on the other side congratulated the rider or tuner, he'd say "Wasn't much. Can't take much tuning to beat a Harley/Indian" (cross out whichever doesn't apply).

Of course there were the jokes. If you saw an Indian being towed in by a Harley, you'd say, "Gosh, how nice of that Indian rider to push the Harley with that stiff rope." And again, it fits either side.

There's a consensus here, with veterans from both sides saying that first the Sport Scout, especially the 648 Big Base, was marginally faster than the Harley WR. The WR was stronger and could be tuned to higher levels of stress. Back on the other side, there was just the one production run of the 648, in 1948, and the actual true Sport Scout went out of production when the war began and never came home, so to speak. Harley-Davidson meanwhile was building all the WRs and WRTTs that the dealers wanted, a couple hundred at least.

So the record shows that Indian won more races in terms of numbers, especially the sprint races, and Harleys won the longer events.

If there's a tribute to this segment of this era, its that the Big Base 648 remained competitive for so long, while the Harleys, BSAs, Nortons, and Triumphs should, by the book, have taken over. "We didn't lose the edge, " says tuner Ralph Farmen, "until we ran out of parts."

The Sportsmen

For every rider with natural talent who took out a license and went pro, there must have been dozens, maybe even hundreds, who raced and competed where they could, on what they had, just for the fun or adventure or challenge, no matter which brand.

Well, the brand did matter. At this third level it seems to have mattered more. The general reason goes back to social pressure, as in the motorcyclist was considered a nut and a social problem. *Indian News* tried to deal with this with anecdotes about the rider who's told he can't be one of them, he's too neat and clean and polite, while he politely says, "I am also a motorcyclist."

So there were the clubs with their pool tables and bowling teams, and the AMA organized tours, in which everybody rode to some place and competed in field meets, rode on planks and tossed tires at targets, or took all the boots and piled them at one end of the field and had a free-for-all won by the first to get his boots back on and win a foot race. Or, how many times could you kick-start your engine in one minute? (More than 60 times, just in case anybody wants to win a trivia contest.)

At the top of this third level were the TTs, enduros, and hillclimbs. The rules were sort of informal and there were classes for a variety of machines, so the riders could run whatever they had.

This led to some surprises. For example, an Indian fancier named Max Bubeck, who clearly had the talent to race professionally but was busy with

Some similar things are more different than they first appear. This is Paul Allbrecht and what the files say is a WRTT, which should be the road racing model except that it doesn't have brakes. All the pro riders had pictures like this on file with the AMA, so a guy couldn't cross the country and ride on somebody else's pro license. © *Harley-Davidson Motor Company*

This is Leo Anthony, at the Milwaukee track on the same day (unless that chap in the background only owns the one dark suit, ditto the man and woman and the sweepers). Anthony is listed as being on a WRL, but check that frame: it's got two front down tubes where Allbrecht's has one, and there on the left grip, a lever! This model is an experiment, a WR with a hand clutch and foot shift. Indian wasn't the only factory with an eye on the future. © *Harley-Davidson Motor Company*

work and women, won the 1947 Greenhorn Enduro, the major West Coast off-road contest, on his Indian Four. True, it was modified, fortified, and equipped with accessory telescopic forks, and the next two machines in were Harley Knucklehead 61s, so there must have been a need for beef and power in the dirt then. But even so, crossing the desert off road with a 500 pound road bike took some doing and some talent.

Leaders of the Pack

To read the accounts and talk to those who were there is to realize quickly that a major part of the legend and the feud came from the work (so to speak) of two men who, not quite in tandem, stoked the fires of the rivalry.

Sam Pierce fought against Harley-Davidson, by his own count, for 42 years. His first motorcycle was a Scout, in 1926, and he raced it, crossed the country, and used it for the carnival ride, the Wall of Death, when he needed money to eat.

His official form would have said designer, as Pierce worked for various car companies in that field, but his major contribution was to be decades ahead of his time. He found and collected and cataloged parts, old Indian parts, years before anybody else considered such a thing (nostalgia wasn't nearly as profitable then as it is now.)

Pierce put together a company fronting all the parts and, because he was mechanically skilled, he could revise, improvise, and improve. Just about the time the make and its owners needed such a person, Sam Pierce was Mr. Indian.

He had a wicked sense of humor and of course Harley-Davidson was the object of his jokes. He painted his trash barrels Team Harley's orange and black, called the Milwaukee firm beer makers and their products 800-pound stoves, that sort of thing.

Because the Indian owners were a club and knew each other and traded wisdom, Pierce's barbs were common knowledge and the new guys learned that mocking Hardly-Ableson (sorry, that just slipped out) was How To Do It.

Why Mr. Indian did this, nobody ever knew, because he didn't seem to have an actual grudge. Rollie Free, on the other hand, had a grudge.

Free is best known in motorcycling circles as the man in the poster, the do-or-die rider stretched flat out, in bathing suit and sneaks, trailing like Linus' blanket behind the Vincent Black Shadow that was clocked at 150.31 miles per hour at Bonneville on September 13, 1948. Free was wearing only the bathing suit because his leathers had flapped earlier in the session and he reasoned, correctly, that the flapping was costing power and speed.

Free wanted to set the record to no small degree because doing so, on a private machine not backed by the Vincent factory, would take the national motorcycle speed record away from the 1936 Knucklehead. And by Rollie Free's reckoning, he and H-D would be evened up, after 25 years.

There was never any question where Free got his grudge against Harley-Davidson. In 1923 he'd bought a racing Harley for the 100-mile national at Kansas City. In the race, his machine wasn't as fast as the factory team. Free said he'd been promised it would be. There were shouts, accusations, and lawsuits. By his account, Free lost. So he went to work for Al Crocker, himself no Harley fan, as a tuner and salesman.

If there's anything to make a motorcycle nut wish for a working Way-Back Machine, it has to be that way back when, it was clear who had the better or faster machine. The contestants went out of town to the open road and held 'em open. Simple, fair and, well some of the time, legal, and even when it wasn't, who was to know?

Rollie Free was a world champion street racer. Before there was such a term, he'd mastered the art of blueprinting: taking the engine apart and making sure every piece was precisely the weight and size and

*V*intage racing has inspired scores of Sport Scouts, like this one, that are fitted with modern tires and faster than they were when new. *Jeff Hackett*

*T*he enduros were for big men on big bikes. This is the famous Jack Pine enduro in 1946, and prudence dictates idling your Knucklehead across the stream, otherwise it swamps and you have to push. © *Harley-Davidson Motor Company*

shape the blueprints called for, ditto all clearances and torquing of the components.

The average machine was close enough for mass production, so to speak, which isn't as good as the craftsmanship Free performed. He set class records on Daytona's Beach and time and again his Indians outran the Harleys, even when they had bigger or newer engines.

The real legend came because Free was contentious. Hollywood and *Life* magazine took some liberties with the Hollister raid that became the Marlon Brando movie, but in fact, there really were guys like the Lee Marvin character who sucker-punched the Brando character. And some of them rode Harleys.

Remember, the guy in high school who the bullies left alone even though they were bigger than he was? They left him alone because he'd made it crystal clear that beating him up would be more trouble than it was worth.

That was Rollie Free. Plus, he was a tremendous storyteller and a born showman. He'd goad the

Harley man into putting up money, refuse to shake hands because that was for gentlemen and no Harley rider was one, then he'd up the stakes and offer to take his wife on the back, and then he'd win the race. And he'd let every Indian rider in whatever state it was hear all about it.

None of the above is to criticize. Free never cheated, and not once in 25 years does the record show anybody getting hurt. That wasn't the point or the intention. Free served on AMA's competition committee, and if there's anything in the record he would have wanted hushed up, it's probably the time he and Walter Davidson took the same side on an issue. (It was to have the races refereed by somebody with no obligation to Indian or Harley, so it would have been difficult not to agree, but the point remains.)

The moral here is that while Clark Gable was teaching moviegoers how to be a gambler, a patriot, and a gentleman all at once, so did Rollie Free teach a generation of Indian owners how to talk about Humbly-Bumblesons. That was the last one, I promise..

The Better-Than Street Racers

If Rollie Free had a weak point, it was that he was fighting below his weight, as they say. A WLD rider who'd chopped off the mufflers and added a fox tail was hopelessly outclassed against Free's tuned Sport Scout before he'd turned on the fuel tap.

There's a better way to test the speed records. Even back then, California was famous for motorcycling enthusiasm and expertise. The gifted amateurs ran the TTs, hillclimbs, and field meets. They also ran at the dry lakes, which are just what they sound like, with hard, flat dirt surfaces. The Air Force took the best spots, but even after the war, heck unto the present day, there were dry lakes open to the public, which became clubs, motorcycles and cars, with really accurate timing systems and fair-and-free rules; most of the time the class was simply for engine displacement.

There was open rivalry on the lakes, witness the photo of Max Bubeck holding his head in mock despair because he'd lost top speed of the day to a

Harley by fractions of a second. When telling the tale Bubeck is careful to remind the listener that the Harley ran early in the day when the air was cool and thick, and he ran in the hot afternoon and he'd ridden to the dry lake while the Harley was hauled. The defeat still hurts, in short.

Even so, Indian racked up some victories. The best belongs to Bubeck. The careful reader's

*B*ig bikes worked. This is Max Bubeck on his 1939 Indian four at the finish of the Cactus Derby. He was eighth on this occasion, although he won the event later and won other enduros on the big four. *Max Bubeck*

*S*ammy Pierce was a designer and stylist for the car companies but more than that, he was Mr. Indian to a generation of Indian fans. He collected parts, literature, and other Indian bits back when they didn't mean anything to anyone, and the faithful are indebted to the man. Pierce was also a master of Harley put-downs. If Pierce didn't invent the joke, he surely knew it and told it so well his listeners never forgot it. *Cycle World*

*T*he small mufflers on this Sport Scout were fitted because there are now noise limits for racing. *Jeff Hackett*

notes will reflect that the standard Scout used the Chief frame so the Scout buyer could install the larger engine later. Bubeck and Chase did that, plus. They used a 101 Scout frame, which was lighter. They stretched it in places and then installed a Chief engine: the bigger twin could be shoehorned into the frame with stock wheelbase and shortened front mounts, but that put the engine too far forward in the frame for what Bubeck and Chase had in mind.

The Chief engine was stroked to displace 78.88 cubic inches, same as the later Chief 80 would be. It got the two-lobe camshafts. They persuaded a welder friend to open the rear cylinder and route the intake port to the side rather than the front, then they bolted on two big carburetors.

The engine was given precise tuning, as in making perfectly sure the ignition cam for the second cylinder fired at exactly the same time as the front cylinder did. Bubeck says you'd be surprised to know how far off they usually were. They rigged an oxygen tank to help the desert air and picked a single, tall gear.

On the day of the run, Bubeck was so busy optimizing the spark setting from the saddle that he

never cracked the oxygen supply, and the gearing was high but they didn't dare because the best time was 135.58 miles per hour, the best ever and still the record for an unstreamlined Indian.

OK, the Harley fans are mumbling from the back of the grandstand, That's one.

There were scores being kept. On the day of that meet in 1948, the timing association reported that 44 Indians of all sizes and types were running, and their average for the meet was 97.08 miles per hour. On the same day, 66 Harley-Davidsons of all sizes and models were running, and no mention was

made of overhead valve. The H-D average was 91.94 miles per hour. Indian won the speed contest and Harley led the sales race.

Level Four:
The Base of the Pyramid

Market research from a much later day reveals that when an enthusiast is in the market for a motorcycle, car, truck, stereo set, or whatever, the prospective buyer reads all the tests and reports. After making the purchase, the new owners read only the reports and tests on the model they chose; or they skip to the

The Sport Scout's basic parts, the two-piece frame and girder forks, look right and work well 60 years later. Jeff Hackett

kee fairgrounds. Ralph Farman confirms it. "The problem wasn't the racers, it was the fans. The Harley or Indian guys wouldn't even sit in the same section. Every so often they'd get mixed up, and have to be escorted out."

Not to lay blame, but the racer attitude seems more useful.

Anybody been wondering how and why Bill Tuman could help the Harley rider?

"Between races I worked for the Harley dealer in Rockford, Illinois. We got along well. He liked my work, and I liked his money."

*R*ollie Free, on the occasion of setting a bunch of class records at Daytona Beach, 1938. Free was a brave and outspoken racer and tuner who liked nothing better than out-doing the Harleys at whatever was being done. *Hap Alzina Archives*

*R*ider Bobby Hill and tuner Dick Gross were part of what was known postwar as the Indian Wrecking Crew. Like Harley's wrecking crew of the 1920s, the Indians didn't always win, but they were always the guys to beat. The big-base Scout, the 648, was one of the best investments Indian ever made. *Don Emde*

bottom of the comparison test and then, if the winner is the one they bought, they read the rest.

It's perfectly natural for the tuners and riders to be rivals and friends, often united against their common foe, the referee or promoter or rule maker. Guys who play for the Giants don't get their arms tattooed because next year, it might be the Cubs.

For motorcycle owners, it's another matter. They've made their choices and even if an owner used to ride an Ossa, he'll still defend his Husqvarna now. Thus, while Ed Kretz could work on his Indian in Harley's shop, Bill Tuman says the only time he got booed was at the Milwau-

There were only 50 full 648 big-base Scouts made by the factory. There were thousands of civilian and military Sport Scouts, and lots of them, hundreds is more like it, were made into racing machines. It was legal, of course. *Jeff Hackett*

*L*ook below the left side of the front cylinder. There's a boss on the case below the cylinder. That's where they stamp the identifying numbers. On factory 648s, the boss is much thicker than on production Scouts and Sport Scouts. There was no official reason ever given for this, but a good guess is that because back then the AMA required the rider to own the engine and to race the engine he qualified with, it was useful sometimes to have, well, ways to make sure the numbers were what they were supposed to be, even if you had to shave the boss down and start over. *Jeff Hackett*

$\mathcal{E}$d Kretz has just been clocked at 114 miles per hour on his Chief at a public, albeit isolated, road. The guys used to gather there on Sundays and run top speed, with clocks. They were otherwise well behaved and the police saw no need to butt in. *Max Bubeck*

$\mathcal{T}$he dry lakes were legal and the perfect place to run for speed. This is Bubeck, tucked down on the tank of his record-setting Chout, a Scout with Chief engine. The timers are at the right, with certified, world-class equipment. *Max Bubeck*

The Chout, a stretched Scout frame with enlarged Chief engine stuffed into it. The heads have been reworked to allow two carburetors, the foot pegs are set back and high, the throttle is on Indian's classic left side, and the telescopic forks are from Vard, an accessory maker. *Max Bubeck*

Bill Tuman, on his 648 with right-side throttle. His mood here is calm and confident but with an air of concern, as if he knows somehow that although Indian will win as long as the parts and the rules hold up, they won't. *Bill Tuman*

159

Chapter Eighteen

The Hydra-Glide, the Arrow, and the New Scout

Harley Shines while Indian Declines

When Indian's new president, management, and design staff stonewalled the furious dealers and refused to put the Scouts back in production, they weren't being stubborn. They were making a classic and ultimately fatal mistake.

Harley-Davidson serves as background here. H-D had noted the interest in motorcycles and the need for a youth model and introduced the 125cc single-cylinder Hummer, which sold well at first. Harley also continued the W series pretty much as it had been before the war. The Model E overhead valve 61 was joined by the F and FL, the overhead valve engine enlarged to 74 cubic inches, while the old V and U sidevalve big twins were dropped.

The joke has long been that the Harley-Davidson motto was, If It Ain't Broke, Don't Fix It. And there has been some of that. More accurately, though, the slogan should be something about One Step at a Time. H-D's engineers had done their war service and had learned some useful stuff, while the company's entire history taught looking before leaping.

Take metallurgy, for instance. In model year 1948 the E and F twins, the 61 and 74, got new cylinder heads. They were made of aluminum alloy, lighter and cooler running than iron. The material had proven itself earlier, with the sidevalve 45s, but

an overhead valve head is a more intricate casting, so they didn't do it until they figured they could do it right. And the new heads had hydraulic damping between the cam lobes and the rockers, so they didn't need to be adjusted.

The rockers and springs were fully enclosed by a cover that looked, to some, like a baking pan, which led to the new engine being nicknamed Panhead, a name which continues to this day.

Once the early problems with the new top end were cured, the big twins got telescopic front suspension for model year 1949. The engineers hadn't doubted its usefulness or the need, they simply had to wait until they could afford to do it.

And the FL got the name Hydra-Glide, the first named Harley since the Sport Twin.

The Imports Landed

There were several new arrows still in Harley-Davidson's quiver, but we need to keep in context here. The wartime calculations by H-D and Indian, expecting new buyers and a challenge from overseas, had been correct.

The English were in deep financial trouble and in typical plucky fashion began working their way out by selling surplus and new sporting bikes. They began

One of the (few) high points of the overhead valve Scout's history was that Max Bubeck rode one and did well. He's the helmeted guy with the grin, the scaff, and the girl. To his left is an Ariel twin, and next to the Ariel is a Harley big twin. There were classes for just about everything in off-road races then. Max Bubeck

*H*arley-Davidson's major postwar project was a new top end for the E and F series twins. The new cylinder heads were aluminum alloy, not cast iron, and they completely enclosed the valve gear. The factory's cutaway drawing shows the single, four-lobe camshaft and the hydraulic valve lifters, done before even Cadillacs had such features. And it's easy to see why the new engine was called the Panhead. © *Harley-Davidson Motor Company*

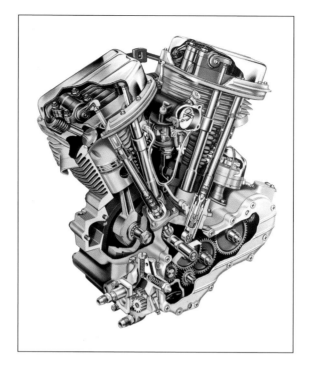

A cutaway drawing of Indian's new twin shows lots of English influence, especially in the exhaust camshaft in front of the cylinders and the intake camshaft behind them, with enclosed pushrods angled up to the rockerboxes. The two pistons went up and down together, with alternate power impulses: Later the Japanese would have the pistons alternate up and down, with staggered power but better balance. The Indian twin was modern but it wasn't strong enough for the job. *Cycle World*

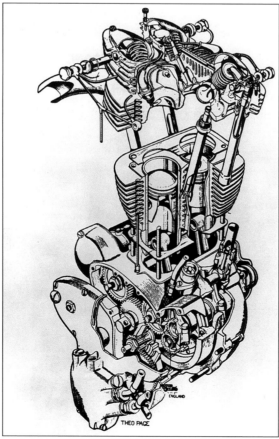

with bargain prices. In 1949 the pound sterling was devalued, which reduced the price of English goods a whole lot and Triumphs and MGs were even more popular. By the late 1940s and early 1950s, the imports had a major share of the U.S. market.

To their shame, Harley-Davidson reacted in shabby fashion, by ordering dealers not to sell other brands, no matter if the models didn't compete.

Some dealers complied. Some, the Canadian branch for instance, refused. The policy made no sense to them because many dealers were in small and isolated towns, to the point Indian shops stocked Harley parts and vice versa. To the Canadians' credit, they backed the factory down.

(In Harley's defense, several of the countries whose products were being sold tariff-free in the U.S. had stiff trade barriers themselves, so we couldn't do to them what they were doing to us. Even so, that's not the fault of the dealer network.)

Indian's Best-Laid Plans

What follows is all the more painful because in theory, Indian's plans were more fair, nevermind being firmly based on the principles of the free market. For this we need to pop in the Indian cassette and rewind to 1944.

G. Briggs Weaver had been chief engineer at the DuPont car company and had worked with Paul du Pont on marine engines before that. That experience and his work on the Indians during the 1930s shows a man qualified for his job. In 1944, Weaver left Indian to work for another company, one with some notions of introducing another American motorcycle. He designed a series of models, powered by a single, a twin, and a four, all done as a module, that is, the same pistons, rods, valves and so forth, in multiples.

Then, in another one of those financial feats of legermain so confusing to the layman, du Pont sold his interest in Indian, and Ralph Rogers bought control, while more-or-less in parallel taking in the outfit that had plans for getting into the motorcycle business. This brought Weaver back into, well, not quite the fold. Same brand, different spread, different foreman. Rogers had done his homework and research, and he was open to the notion that what America was waiting for was a refined, cultured, lightweight motorcycle.

When Indian management had the rent-a-cops bar the door on the Indian dealers who wanted the Scout back, it wasn't that they didn't believe in middleweights. To the contrary. Indian was betting the family fortune, future, and honor on light-weights and middleweights. The family cow was riding, so to speak, on magic beans: the faith that the new designs would work and that they were what the non-motorcycling public was waiting for.

The New School

One of the ways design history repeats itself is the story of the Visionary and the Grump. One member of the team is brilliant, daring, intuitive . . . and goes too far. The other half is practical, cautious, and lacks imagination. One half is the sails, driving into the future and the other half is the keel that keeps the ship upright.

Paul du Pont's son Lex, who was there, says that Weaver had vision and the willingness to grab bulls he couldn't throw. Paul du Pont meanwhile, was keenly practical. Weaver's departure must not have been personal, because Lex du Pont says Weaver came to show Paul du Pont the plans for the modular engines. du Pont approved the idea, had in fact been working on the same principle, but told Weaver his design wouldn't hold up. Lex du Pont says Edward Turner, the brilliant Englishman behind the legendary Triumph Speed Twin, was in the neighborhood and said the same thing. Weaver didn't agree.

The new Indian president Rogers knew production, finance, marketing, and promotion, but he wasn't an engineer. Rogers approved the designs and the concepts and committed Indian to a massive conversion, with the company's future riding on a radical revision of what the American motorcycle was supposed to be.

The initial design called for a single, displacing 10.5 cubic inches, a twin of 21 cubic inches, and a four with 42 cubic inches. All were overhead valve, that

concept having been accepted by everybody by this time, with laggards holding back only because they didn't have the money or didn't have a design ready.

Before the engines were built, somebody realized they'd be short on power, so the multiples became 13, 26, and 52 cubic inches. The Chief had gone back into limited production by this time (1947 and 1948), which took care of the big-bike market, and the plan was to expand the market with the smaller models.

The single was coded 149 and named the Arrow, while the vertical twin was 249 and called Scout. Both were almost completely modern, with hand clutch, footshift, and foot pegs instead of floorboards. Front suspension was telescopic forks on both, while the twin had plunger rear hub standard, and the Arrow's basic model had rigid rear wheel and plunger hub as an option.

There was no lack of planning. The hope was to attract new people, all those who told the surveyors that they liked the idea of motorcycling, it was that the motorcycles were so big, and loud, and well, ridden by the rough element.

And then H-D opened up both barrels so to speak, with telescopic forks, hand clutch, and foot shift to go with the Panhead engine, and they had a new name: Hydra-Glide. The rectangular chrome thing on the frame tube just below the front of the tank is helper spring, because working the clutch was work for the average hand. The helper is known as a Mousetrap because that's what it looks like.
© *Harley-Davidson Motor Company*

*I*mpressive, eh? The Hydra-Glide was as big and strong as it looked, especially when fitted with the accessories like the spotlights and crashbars and the chrome-plated toolbox on the rear of the frame. *Roy Kidney/Vintage Museum*

*T*he Arrow deserved better than it got. Indian's own entry-level motorcycle was neat, compact, and attractive. It was mostly modern, with telescopic forks, hand clutch, and foot shift (on the left, which is sort of odd, what with Indian's earlier preference for the right). This is the basic model, with a rigidly mounted rear wheel. A sprung hub was an option. The single's relationship to the twin can be seen by the splayed pushrods, front and back. *Bob Stark*

FAR RIGHT
*H*istory is full of surprises. This very machine, and don't worry about the missing or chopped fenders, is *the* prototype Indian Scout, built and tested in 1946. Later research showed the tester reported major damage and problems in the first day's ride, but that this report of the flaws was ignored. *The Shop*

No small portion of Indian's investment in the program involved advertising the new models and motorcycling in places where motorcycles had seldom been seen. There were celebrities. Actress Jane Russell—ask your granddad—race driver Rex Mays, band leader Vaughn Munroe, even cowboy star Roy Rogers, who rode an Indian Four with the Indian M. C. of Milwaukee, speaking of shipping rice to Japan, all appeared in ads and in ostensibly impartial magazines.

Speaking of that, *Indian News,* formerly the voice of Indian riders, in 1947 threw open the doors, adopting the slogan "For every motorcyclist and his family."

Yes, the editors said inside, *Indian News* "is more concerned with Indian than with other makes...but what it (the magazine) is most interested in, is the now inevitable growth of the motorcycling sport."

There was a tremendous awareness, inside and out. In 1947 there were aftermarket kits to swap the hand controls for foot, and vice versa. There was a popular front suspension made by a company

named Vard, which allowed installation of telescopic forks on both Indians and Harleys.

The concept, getting new people into the sport and filling a changing set of customers wishes, was correct. That's what hurts the most.

The ad campaign and public relations efforts and the actual designs were only parts of a whole. Indian had acquired a new plant, with all the necessary equipment. There had been tours of the dealerships to lure the better businessmen into the fold and sort them from the old guys who wouldn't go along. There had been projections of production costs and

such to make sure the Arrow and Scout would bring in modest profits for the dealers and the factory. And there had been money borrowed on the strength of all this working according to plan. That's a broad hint.

The Arrow and the new Scout went into production July 15, 1948. There were no objective tests in those days so it's no surprise to find the news accounts, wink and nudge, beginning with praise for Rogers and the team and closing with the claim that "you can't hurt" the new Indian.

From a historical prospective the Arrow and the Scout were basically good ideas, carried out with reasonable skill and good intentions. They were modern. They were also small, partly because the European motorcycles with which the Indians were to compete were scaled to their riders (before the western world got enough to eat, Europeans were on average smaller than the Yanks).

According to the brochure, the Arrow and Scout were built with a nominal wheelbase of 53 1/2 inches.

The Arrow's weight was listed as 245 pounds, the Scout's as 280. That sounds as if they'd been weighed minus fuel, oil, or air in the tires, but that's what brochures have always been famous for. Arrow and Scout "are not little motorcycles, " the brochure went on. "They don't look little and they don't act little." Rekindling the spirit of the original Indian, the booklet says "The combination of war-born metallurgy, American know-how, and high-speed, high-compression engines has resulted in machines that deliver more horsepower per pound of weight, more horsepower per cubic inch, and consequently more brilliant performance than any motorcycles ever built before, anywhere in the world."

Then came, well, call it an upside-down pyramid. At the very broadest part of the debacle, the campaign simply fell on uninterested ears and eyes. The vast public didn't want motorcycles, not even if the motorcycles were small and neat and efficient. Motorcycles weren't yet in fashion, which is the force that drives the world.

The rampaging success of the VW Beetle and Honda Civic made no sense to the men who'd refused to make small cars because they'd seen the Austin, the Bantam, and the Crosley fail, despite the surveys in which people said they wanted small cars.

Thus, just because Honda and Yamaha took over the world motorcycle markets in the 1950s and 1960s doesn't mean Indian could sell small bikes in the 1940s, nor could Harley-Davidson in the 1950s.

Next, the public having failed to react well, there were those who did buy the new Indians, which promptly blew up. This can be debated, in the sense that there are those who bought the new Scouts and found them just fine. Some seem to have been reliable. But the anecdotes tell of piles of junked engines shipped back to the factory by the dealers—probably the same guys who demanded the return of, as Coca-Cola put it, the Classic Sport Scout.

Paul Dupont and Edward Turner had been right. The new engines didn't have the strength nor the oiling capacity needed to match their output. On average, the new-style buyers who putted to shop and school didn't have trouble. It was the old-style

Indian fans, the ones used to big understressed engines that ran at speed on the open road hour after hour, who suffered the blowups.

At the next level down, the projections and estimates on costs and how they'd be used to set the retail price of the new models were woefully incorrect in, as you guessed, the wrong direction. The factory was losing money on every sale, even before the warranty claims flooded in.

As an adjunct to that, the British pound sterling was devalued, meaning the English motorcycles were cheaper here, and the Indians were more expensive over there. The Indian Motocycle Com-

The new Scout looked the part, that is, new. There was suspension front and rear, overhead valves, foot shift and hand clutch, fully valanced fenders, all in keeping with the fashion and engineering of the time. *Jerry Greer*

The frame is filled with engine, a virtual requirement as noted earlier, and the dual exhausts have an attractive sweep. The only flaw in the looks department may be that the machine itself was just a fraction smaller than the American public expected a sporting twin to be. *Jerry Greer*

The bulk and the strength of the motorcycle sport, then if not now, was the small-town dealer. In almost every case, the dealer was his own man, which George Beerup, shown here in front of his Harley store, must have been. These men would help you if they liked you, and they didn't need your money if they thought you didn't deserve one of their machines. And, any time somebody doubts there's such a thing as a paternal instinct, show 'em this photo. *Jerry Greer*

pany's annual report for 1947 shows a modest loss for the year but says the new models that are on the way will do well in the export market. As they might have done, if, if, if.

The pointed edge of this pyramid begins with one of the odder facts in the story. Grumbling legend says that Harley and Indian took over the AMA and rigged the racing so the dumb old side-valve 750s would rule over the martyred overhead valve 500s, right?

So here's Indian, and they're going to make an overhead valve twin and they make no move to remove the presumed handicap. Not only that, they build their overhead valve twin with 436cc, giving away 13 percent of what they could have had free.

Some dictatorship that was. Indian, plainly, was not telling the AMA or the racers what to do.

As Miss Piggy would say, "Au contraire." Parallel to the work on the overhead valve twins, Indian produced and delivered the 648s, the big-base Scouts filtered to the favored few. Sport Scout riders won the two biggest events of 1946 (the full season wasn't possible so soon after the war's end), and in 1947 one of the prelegal 648s won the Daytona 200, which even then was the motorcycle race that was sure to make all the papers.

That same year Max Bubeck won the Greenhorn Enduro on his four, which incidentally had benefited from his revisions to the lubrication system; stock, there simply wasn't enough oil going to the right places.

More important here, the 1947 Laconia saw 19 finishers. Eleven were on Harleys and seven rode Indians, with Ted Edwards' second place the only Indian in the top ten. The very next day, historian Hatfield says, Indian authorized work on the real 648s, the 50 required to make the model legal. Clearly it was more practical to hedge the bet than to change the rules.

The new Scout was in the background. Floyd Emde won the Daytona 200 in 1948 aboard a 648, and the year's total Indian wins are too numerous to list here. And then Indian put its money where its investment was. The Arrow and Scout were subject to all the revisions they could invent, while one of the easiest was to enlarge the twin.

Perhaps because the use of the name had created resentment, the Scout badge was dropped from the overhead valve twin for 1949. The bore was enlarged, from 2.38 inches to 2.54, so displacement was now close to the legal racing limit of 500cc.

The badge now read Warrior TT. The new model wasn't ready for Daytona 1949, where Kretz's 648 was fractionally slower than the winning Norton 500 single and then retired.

To set the stage here: one of the AMA's top attractions in the 1940s was the Gypsy Tour, usually a weekend of racing or sport, to which all the clubs

rode for a big get-together. One of the favorites tours was to the races at Laconia, New Hampshire, a resort and beach town with a challenging gravel-and-asphalt road course.

To let the public know about the new Warrior, the factory arrived at Laconia 1949 with no fewer than 12 sponsored and professionally prepped machines. And they all broke down, while thousands of fans, Indian and Harley-Davidson, looked on. The official history says the magnetos broke, which is possible since the Harley-Davidson magnetos, until the early 1970s, were famous for getting weak when the going got tough.

But all twelve? One of the rules in racing, back when the factory made the engines and somebody else supplied the electrics, was for the engine to grenade on the straight, air filled with flying pistons and rods, and then the rider would

*N*ot to argue against modern technology and black boxes, but once upon a time, if the oil feed on your Indian four clogged while you were riding around in the desert, you could stop, lay the bike on its side, whip out the tool kit, find and fix the problem, and ride it home. *Max Bubeck*

*S*portsmanship: This is 1946 and the winners of their classes in the Cactus Derby have gathered at Fordyce Harley-Davidson in Riverside, California, to pick up their trophies. Some of the guys (OK, there's one girl, in the center of the front row) have worn their Indian jerseys to the Harley store, and they're still alive. *Max Bubeck*

look the camera right in the lens and say the ignition failed.

Plainly, this doesn't matter now. Then as now, what was important was that at the very bottom of our upside-down pyramid, the new Indian, the model on which the company's future had been wagered, had appeared at its very worst in front of the very audience Indian needed to impress.

Disaster. Debacle. Words fail to convey how bad this was. Unless the words are that Ed Kretz became a Triumph racer and dealer. And that Hap Alzina, the guy who picked up Indian's payroll back when he still had hope, took on the BSA distributorship for the West Coast.

Our inverted pyramid, all those fans in the shops and at the trackside, rooting for the grassroots racers who emulated and copied the professionals who worked for and with the factory men and officials at the top, had just pinched itself shut.

*I*ndian's last major (but not the last national) victory came in 1948, when Floyd Emde, who'd earlier won fame riding Harleys, won the Daytona 200 at record speed on his old-style Scout, owned by the San Diego dealer and tuned by the shop foreman. *Don Emde*

*T*he Warrior TT was a better overhead valve Scout, with the engine enlarged to 500cc, the class limit. The high pipes known as TT pipes and used by Harley, Triumph, and later Honda to tell the public the bike had sporting inclinations—improved the looks of the bike. But it wasn't all that fast, and the earlier Scout's reputation and lack of money for improvements or marketing dragged the project down. *Roy Kidney*

In their later years, the Harley FL, left, and Indian Chief had grown, literally, to look alike and to define their time. They were also works of art. *Jeff Hackett*

Chapter Nineteen

The Final Hours

Just as your grandmother warned you, just about the time the Indian enthusiast had to be saying, "Well, things can't get worse," things got worse. And yup, it was deja vu all over again. When the Arrow and Scout took longer to make and cost more and had problems, when the cash ran low, Indian's new owners did what they had done before: they borrowed money. When the borrowed money ran out, Indian made another of those decisions that looked right at the time.

Indian's marketing strategy called for persuading the non-motorcycling public to become the motorcycling public. It made sense for Rogers to sign up Indian, with its dealer network, with an English company. Indian dealers would sell imports, giving them something besides the Chief to offer while the Arrow and Scout were discontinued and the Warrior was on the drawing boards.

It didn't work. Instead, the manufacturing division couldn't make the loan payments and the new partners took control, but not completely. Indian Motocycle Company was cut in half, in effect. The British partners, who simply wanted to sell motorcycles in the United States and didn't care what the motorcycles were nor where they were made, took over the sales and distribution half.

The manufacturing portion of Indian remained in Springfield but under the control of one of the companies that had been part of the industrial conglomerate built by Rogers before he jumped into the briar patch known as motorcycling.

There were some flickers of light. The unquenchable Max Bubeck won the Cactus Derby enduro in 1950 on his Warrior TT; typically, Bubeck stoutly maintains there was nothing wrong with the Warrior that a little fettling and care wouldn't fix. And Bill Tuman took two nationals that same year on his Big Base Scout.

Just to close out the racing record, Hatfield was told by Tom Sifton, the best of the Harley tuners, that there were three Indian tuners, Dick Gross, Art Hafter, and Tuman, who'd built Scouts faster than his (Sifton's) Harley WR.

The last Indian win of an AMA national came in 1953, with Ernie Beckman at Williams Grove, Pennsylvania. And the very last major Indian win went to (who else?) Bubeck and his Warrior at the Greenhorn Enduro in 1962. Wow.

In the Long Run

The run was over. The manufacturing company did what little could be done: they kept the Warriors

Hard Times Department. This is the showroom of Johnson Motors in Los Angeles. When Indian hit the financial ropes because all the money had been spent on the ill-fated singles and twins, Indian dealers were expected to sell imports, English ones, right along with the domestic models. Thus, on the stand at the far left is an out-of-production Indian four, with an Ariel twin behind it, while between the Chief and the Scout is an Ariel Square Four. *Hap Alzina Archives*

*I*ndian didn't quit easy. Here's Max Bubeck again, enlisted in the sales effort because of his racing wins, at a motorcycle show in 1951, telling all who will listen how good the new Warrior is. *Max Bubeck*

coming for a few hundred more examples. The Chief was unique on the market: it was simply the biggest motorcycle and not like anything else. The engine was enlarged to 80 cubic inches, and the plunger rear hub was joined by telescopic forks, and several thousand Chiefs, bearing Roadmaster or Blackhawk badges, were made and sold in the early 1950s.

According to the official reports, the 648 Scouts cost $1,000 each to make. As a deliberate promotional venture, they were priced at $600 to the dealer, so the factory lost $400 on each of the 50 models built to meet the AMA's production rule and lost $20,000 on the project.

The total cost of the modern motorcycle project, the Arrow, Scout, and Warrior, in design and tooling up and promoting and making good and on and on, comes to $6.5 million. That's what it says in the books.

Back to What If for a moment. It's worth noting that there was in fact a modest boom in motorcycling, except that it was the sport not the utility aspect that

brought people in, and it was the imports, mostly English and German, that benefited the most. And there wasn't anything fundamentally wrong with the models that failed. At the same time, it's fair to note that George Weaver and Ralph Rogers resigned, not at the same time by the way, and went to work in other businesses.

It isn't fair to wonder though, not that one can help doing exactly that, what would have happened if the money Indian poured into the Euro-style models had been, well, better spent. Perhaps it would have been better if the Arrow had been revised and the Scout had been kept in production to fill the gap and justify the 648 program, while the ad campaign had been aimed at people who already wanted a motorcycle.

Milwaukee Keeps Moving

I raised the above unfair question because Harley-Davidson came close to doing just that. The 125cc Hummer received improved suspension and then an enlarged engine, 165cc, and there was a tuning program to get lighter riders into the sport.

In 1952, H-D introduced its postwar sports bike, coded Model K for the standard version and KK for the tuned road model. Model KL would have been the normal sequence, but that combination had been used for a secret project, an overhead valve twin never seen in public.

The K was unit construction, with the flywheels, gearbox, camshafts, primary drive all contained in the crankcase's four compartments. It was footshift on the right, while W series and the big twins had always been left-side shifters; obviously the K was supposed to meet and defeat the right-side shifting Brit bikes.

The K's engine was, not that one had to ask, a 45-degree V-twin, fork and blade connecting rods on a single crankpin, with primary on the left and gearcase on the right. In the gearcase was an arc of four one-lobe camshafts, just like the W series general outline, the K engine was simply a W engine, primary drive and gearbox built as a unit instead of three assemblies. The K engine was sidevalve, flathead as they said and still say, just like the W and the Ford V-8.

Why? Hadn't the overhead valve system proved itself? Wasn't overhead valve the way everybody was going if they hadn't already? Wasn't the Harley big twin an overhead valve with alloy heads?

Yes to all the above. It was simply that overhead valve engines cost more to make and were trickier as well and anyway, racing had proved the 750cc sidevalve engine to match the 500cc overhead valve rivals, and the English were selling 500s, so the K Model was a sidevalve 750. It's out of our rivalry's time frame but for the record, the K wasn't as fast as the imports so it

was stroked to 883cc in 1954, and in 1957 H-D came out with the overhead valve Sportster, also 883 but with shorter stroke, larger bore, and lots more power. Harley-Davidson has always known how to progress, it's simply that The Motor Company has to have its arms twisted first. Which is probably why the K had telescopic forks and swingarm rear suspension, then becoming the standard.

The big twin meanwhile became singular in that the 61 panhead was dropped, leaving only the 74, the FL. That model's modernization program

Harley-Davidson was going from strength to strength, witness this gathering of the touring-equipped faithful.
© Harley-Davidson Motor Company

The Model KR is a study in contrast to the KHK on the opposite page. Stripped of all but essentials and equipped with a hotter engine, the KR became Harley-Davidson's Class C weapon.

"I thought you were dead,
Joe Hill," I said.
"I was," he said to me.
—*The Ballad of Joe Hill*,
the story of a folk hero too
proud and stubborn
to stay dead.

was optional footshift and had a clutch in 1952 and (again, out of our time frame) swingarm rear suspension in 1958.

The Effective End

Sorry to spoil one of motorcycling's better legends, but the last Indian Chiefs were not a fleet assembled in 1955 for the New York Police Department, the members of which were so loyal to Indian that they prevailed on Springfield to assemble on final order.

That story has made the rounds since, oh, 1956 at least. Most motorcycle nuts for several generations have heard it, and one can't guess how many root beers were waged on the legend until spoilsport Jerry Hatfield finally asked the guys who were there, and they said, "Sorry, didn't happen."

What did happen is the shrinking staff in the manufacturing half of the former Indian Motocycle Company assembled some Chiefs and Warriors through 1951 and 1952, while building some prototypes and making cosmetic changes, in hopes the sales half was interested.

They weren't.

On December 2, 1953, on stationery headed "The Indian Company. America's Pioneer in Motorcy-

cling" and addressed as "An important message to all dealers," came the following piece of semi-information:

"The management of the Indian company has just completed a study of conditions adversely affecting motorcycle production in the United States. This has led to a decision to suspend assembly of complete motorcycles at Springfield during 1954. The sole purpose of this production holiday is to strengthen the position of the Company for future activities in the motorcycle manufacturing field. . . .

"An intact and aggressive organization is prepared for action as the United States distributor for the top ranking British built motorcycles. Along with our own Indian Brave and Papoose (imports wearing Indian badges) such famous names as Norton, Vincent, Royal Enfield, A.J.S., and Matchless round out our most complete 1954 motorcycle program.

"This program, which will be energetically promoted, is realistic and will make money for every participating dealer. We urge your continued loyal support."

The cynics in the crowd will curl their collective lips and say something along the lines of, "Oh yeah, hope they get the loyalty they earned."

But that's too tough. Instead, the record shows that the Indian Company was effectively finished, done in. Never again would an Indian motorcycle come down the assembly line.

The Revival Myth

This is the history of Harley-Davidson vs. Indian, not the history of either make or of American motorcycles in general. The end of Indian production therefore is the end of the rivalry. It's a sad ending and it's safe to guess that not even Walter Davidson would have been happy to see such a finish to such a great race.

Oh, there were sputters. The English owners juggled and swapped parts and badges for a couple of years until their industry made similar mistakes and came to a similar end. During the dirt bike boom of the 1970s, the owners of the Indian name persuaded Italian two-stroke engines into Taiwanese frames. They were honest machines and performed

While Indian's modern machines were failing, Harley-Davidson eased in the present with the K models. The bikes featured full suspension, foot shifting, hand clutches, unit construction of the engine and gearbox, and an upgraded version of the venerable sidevalve 45-cubic-inch powerplant. *Roy Kidney/Vintage Museum*

This bike is the best of the K series, the KHK. The KHK featured an engine enlarged from 750 to 883 cc and hotter camshafts and improved timing. *Roy Kidney/Vintage Museum*

good service until they, too, were overcome by technology from elsewhere.

Did someone in the back there ask about the revival, make that plural: revivals? Along about 1954, there were people talking that talk, as there are right this minute in 1997. Several. More than one can keep track of, especially as they all seem to run out of steam or money and several revivalists have had serious talks with the various agencies responsible for not letting some chaps mislead, so to speak, other chaps.

Forget it. And even if a whole new team brought out a motorcycle with the grand old name, naming your granddaughter Babe Ruth wouldn't enable her to hit 60 home runs a year, eh?

And yet . . .

Every year at the fairgrounds at Davenport, Iowa, there's a classic and antique motorcycle meet.

*C*lass C was still in the rule book, but Indian and the imports were relegated to second when Harley-Davidson introduced the KR: K for the 750 unit engine, R for racing. The KR powertrain was undeniably based on the K's, but the engine was vastly different internally, all the useful stuff like lights or brakes were gone, and the KR weighed nearly 200 pounds less than the road-going K.

*T*his is a reproduction, built in 1996 by Jerry Greer and commissioned by David Edwards, then editor of *Cycle World*. The machine began as a military bike and was liberated into a racer after the war. Using photos and recollections from the time, Greer built a Sport Scout engine stroked to 57 cubic inches with Chief flywheels. The magneto comes from racing, and the battery has to be charged at home because the generator drive has been sacrificed in the interests of speed. Speaking of which, to be really authentic, Greer and Edwards ran this Scout 100-plus at the dry lakes. *Cycle World*

Best in the country. A bunch of guys show up with the old board track singles and twins, intake-over-exhaust and four-valve.

These old beauties are part of the fastest-growing segment of motorcycle sport, vintage racing. In addition to scores of old machines being dragged from barns and put back on the track, there are thriving companies making perfect replica parts; engine, frames, and whatever else is needed. And the two brands with the biggest catalogs are—you guessed it—Harley-Davidson and Indian.

Every vintage race meet has a class for the hand shift twins and there are right this minute rival tuners building better and faster Big-Base Scouts. To see them in action, out of the turns at full power slide, thunder and flame bellowing from the open pipes, is to know why Joe Hill still lives, in spirit and memory.

As far as the emotional aspect, 40 years after Indian folded, there are still dozens of shops in this country, make that the world, where if you ride up on a Harley you will be asked to to park your engine oil donor somewhere else. It will be said with a smile, but the suggestion will be serious.

Let's hope it's always so.

The tank art? Greer and Edwards knew that many of the postwar riders and racers had been in the Air Force. What could be more natural, then, than to decorate the bike's tank with nose art painting, as seen in combat? The front fender is off and the rear fender has been chopped short, bobbed as they said then, with tiny taillight. The gearshift has been moved back out of the way and is what was called a jockey shift, as if the rider reaches down for more speed.
Cycle World

*W*hat it came to at the curtain was a rolling work of art: the 80-cubic-inch Roadmaster Chief, with suspension, all the touring equipment, lights, chrome, and enclosures the designers could imagine bolted to the basic machine. And not enough people wanted the only model Indian's manufacturing half could afford to make or could make work. *Cycle World/Bob Stark*

Index